Ernest Hemingway

THE
OAK PARK
LEGACY

Ernest Hemingway

THE
OAK PARK LEGACY

Edited by

JAMES NAGEL

THE UNIVERSITY OF
ALABAMA
PRESS

Tuscaloosa and
London

Library of Congress Cataloging-in-Publication Data

Ernest Hemingway : the Oak Park legacy / edited by James Nagel.
p.   cm.
Essays presented at a conference held July 17–21, 1993, in Oak Park, Ill.
Includes bibliographical references (p.   ) and index.
ISBN 0–8173–0842–3
1. Hemingway, Ernest, 1899–1961—Criticism and interpretation—
Congresses.   2. Hemingway, Ernest, 1899–1961—Childhood and
youth—Congresses.   3. Authors, American—20th century—Biography—
Congresses.   4. Oak Park (Ill.)—Biography—Congresses.   I. Nagel, James.
PS3515.E37Z58688   1996
813'.52—dc20   96–5033
CIP

British Library Cataloguing-in-Publication Data available

In memory of

JOHN OLIN EIDSON

CONTENTS

Contents

Hemingway's Later Work:
A Farewell to Oak Park

Afterword

PREFACE

JAMES NAGEL

The essays in this collection, all of them published here for the first time, were presented as part of "Ernest Hemingway: The Oak Park Legacy," a conference held in Hemingway's hometown, July 17–21, 1993, under the sponsorship of The Ernest Hemingway Foundation of Oak Park. Although this volume contains a selection of the papers presented at the program, it cannot attempt to capture the energy and excitement that characterized the entire event, with the presentation of a new play (*Lovely Walloona,* written by Morris Buske) and tours of the Hemingway house, the Oak Park and River Forest High School, and the many Frank Lloyd Wright homes in the community. It was an exciting and informative three days for the hundreds of participants who attended the conference, a joyful tribute to the young man who grew up in this village to become a Nobel laureate for literature.

In addition to the scholars whose essays are here collected, many other people participated in the program and contributed to the informed discussion that enlivened the conference. One of the most intriguing events was a panel discussion devoted to "Hemingway in International Perspective," with Judy Hen (Israel), Xiaoming Huang (People's Republic of China), Carlos Azevedo (Portugal), Kazuhira Maeda (Japan), and Ove G. Swensson (Sweden) as participants. In more formal investigations of Hemingway's works, Joseph Waldmeier, John P. Weber, Robert

Martin, James Steinke, Robert W. Trogdon, Linda Wagner-Martin, Carolyn Poplett, Redd Griffin, Michael Seefeldt, Janice R. Byrne, and Rose Marie Burwell made important contributions in forms that could not be represented here. Scott Schwar, President of The Ernest Hemingway Foundation of Oak Park, supervised local arrangements along with Jeanette Fields, Redd Griffin, and especially Barbara Ballinger, the archivist for the Hemingway Museum. Stephen Plotkin, of the Hemingway Collection at the John F. Kennedy Presidential Library in Boston, discussed the materials in that archive, including the scrapbooks that Grace kept throughout Ernest Hemingway's childhood, and Barbara Ballinger described the extensive collection of family papers donated to the Oak Park museum by Marcelline Hemingway Sanford, Ernest Hemingway's older sister. Marcelline's two sons, John and James Sanford, shared memories of their celebrated uncle. Waring Jones spoke about an important collection of Hemingway manuscripts and letters he donated to the museum, documents now permanently available for scholarly investigation.

In a larger sense, the entire community of Oak Park participated in the celebration with a picnic in the town park and the dedication of the Hemingway birthplace at 339 North Oak Park Avenue as an educational museum. The preservation and restoration of the author's home was a suitable conclusion to the conference and the beginning of a new series of literary events for those interested in the life and works of Ernest Hemingway. In a small gesture of support from the scholars whose essays are here published, the proceeds of this volume will be dedicated to the support of this facility.

HEMINGWAY GENEALOGY

Anson Tyler ⊤ **Adelaide Edmonds**   **Ernest Miller** ⊤ **Caroline Hancock**
  (b. 1844)   (b. 1841)   (b. 1840)   (b. 1843)
           (M. 1867)   (M. 1865)

Anginette (b. 1869)   Ernest (b. 1867)
Clarence Edmonds (b. 1871) ——————— **Grace (b. 1872)**
Willoughby Anson (b. 1874)   Leicester Campbell (b. 1874)
George Roy (b. 1876)
Alfred Tyler (b. 1877)
Grace Adelaide (b. 1881)

                                 (M. 1896)

Marcelline	**Ernest Miller**	Ursula	Madeline	Carol	Leicester
(b. 1898)	(b. 1899)	(b. 1902)	(b. 1904)	(b. 1911)	(b. 1915)

Ernest Hemingway

THE
OAK PARK
LEGACY

Introduction

JAMES NAGEL

The Hemingways
and Oak Park, Illinois:
Background and Legacy

YOUNG WILLYS WAS SICK when Harriet Hemingway opened her
new diary on January 1, 1852, and the next day Dr. Woodruff
came to the house and administered leeches.[1] Testifying to the
efficacy of the treatment, the boy quickly recovered. The Hemingways were living in Plymouth, Connecticut, that year, and they
had a complex family. Harriet was not Allen Hemingway's first
wife; he had married her aunt Marietta in 1833, and that union
had produced five children: Rodney (b. 1835); Riley (b. 1836),
who died at the age of three, the first of many tragedies in a family
with more than its fair share; Mary Ann (b. 1837); Rocelina
(b. 1839); and George (b. 1842), the same year his mother died.
Six months later Allen married Harriet, the daughter of Anson
and Harriet Tyler. So when her own son (the paternal grandfather of Ernest Hemingway) was born on August 26, 1844, she
named him Anson, after her father. Willys followed in 1847, and
a daughter, Harriet Lucretia, in 1850. The Hemingways were
never very inventive about names, using the same ones, or varia-
tions, generation after generation.

With seven children living in the household, and with Allen
established as the postmaster for nearby Terryville in addition to
running the general store, the family would seem to have been
firmly settled. From the indications in Harriet's diary, they knew
everyone for miles around, they were surrounded by relatives,

3

and, as would be true for their descendants, they were pillars of the church. Throughout her diary, Harriet regularly commented on sermons, speeches, and special events of the congregation, such as the temperance lecture in Plymouth on March 19 and the pleasant visit with Deacon Judson in Plymouth Hollow. To counterbalance the ethereal, she also pays persistent attention to the world of the flesh, particularly to her own sensuality and to the sexual misconduct of the villagers. In August 1852, for example, she began a running commentary on the doings of a Mr. Franklin Hall and a Miss Perkins, who had the community abuzz for days, culminating in the loss of a public court case by the hapless Hall. Harriet seems to have observed the proceedings with undue interest: "I feel very unwell tonight owing to the excitement today," she wrote on August 7. The Reverend Richardson's sermon that Sunday concerned adultery, and on September 5, 1852, Harriet observed, "There is a great deal of talk upon that subject in the village at present." A month later she wrote that "Mr. Willard Goodwin has been suspended from the[2] Church on account of misconduct with Mr. Atwater's daughter."

But most of her diary covers the mundane responsibilities of running a large household, with a special stress on travel to neighboring communities (particularly Hartford), her deep love for her husband and children, financial transactions, and her tendency to see her life in historical perspective, observing the anniversaries of significant family events well in the past. She seems to have deeply enjoyed a trip to Boston in September 1852, staying at the Pearl Street Hotel and touring the Museum of Fine Art, and it is clear that it was a buying trip for Allen, restocking the store. She ended her diary for that year on a typically reflective note: "And now the year is about to close and what great reason have we to be thankful that our family have enjoyed very good health the most of the year and that we are all permitted to see the close of this day as well as year. Lord help us all to live as we shall wish we had done when we come to die."

The following year passed in Harriet's diary without major incident, although in October 1853 Harriet bore her last child, Adelbert Porter Hemingway, called "Delly" within the family.

Allen Hemingway sold his cow and hired a German girl to help with domestic duties, and a succession of German and Irish servants moved in and out of the household. In August, Harriet recorded that Anson had been causing trouble for his parents, and a month later the situation was no better: "Anson has been causing us more trouble which makes me feel very sad. Lord help us to bring him up in thy Love and fear."[3]

But 1854 brought an end to this phase of the life of the Hemingway family, for Allen, for the first time, announced his intention to move the family to Illinois: "Mr. Hemingway is quite engaged about going out West to buy a farm for his boys," she wrote on January 18. The motivation for the move seems clearly to have been the need for employment for his sons, for Rodney was already nineteen, George was twelve, and there were three younger boys. Land was expensive in Connecticut, the fields were flinty, the weather uncertain. Opportunity lay in the Midwest, with its level expanse of rich soil. A man with a steady job in Chicago could do worse than to purchase a farm for his boys. Harriet's hesitation about the idea seems to have more to do with her need for her husband's constant companionship than for her devotion to Connecticut, as when she recorded that "Mr. Hemingway is talking some of going to Illinois in the course of a few weeks. I can hardly consent to have him go" (January 26, 1854).

Despite her personal reservations, she helped in the preparations, and on February 13 Allen and Rodney left on the stage-coach, leaving twelve-year-old George in charge of the store. While they were absent, Harriet outlined the details of the journey: "O how glad I am we have received a letter from Mr. Hemingway this evening. They are both well. They stopped at Dunkirk, N.Y. Have had a very pleasant time" (February 18, 1854). Allen returned home in early March, leaving Rodney in Chicago, and set about selling the New England property, much to Harriet's dismay: "I do feel very bad to leave our House and Sell the most of our things" (March 9, 1854). To get the troublesome Anson out of the way, his parents sent him to spend several months on the farm of Uncle Baldwin, his mother recording that "I think it will be [good] for his health to be on a farm. It is hard to part with him" (March 14, 1854). Allen sold the house to William McKey and another place at the East Church to Dr. Whitmore and Mr. McKey, and on April 3 Allen departed again for Illinois: "Mr. Hemingway left home this morning for Chicago. I hope he will arrive there Safe and find Rodney well. O how lonely I do feel when I get ready for bed." When Allen had not returned three months later, Harriet was clearly eager for their reunion: "Oh how I long to see him," she wrote on July 6. The following week her prayers were answered when her husband returned.

This family turmoil seemed to take its toll on Allen, and Harriet feared that she had made him ill: "I made some remarks which caused him to feel very bad and both of us have shed many tears. I am very sorry and will try to guard my tongue better" (July 28, 1854). But he apparently needed to return to Illinois to complete negotiations, for he left again on August 16 and wrote back two weeks later that he had purchased a small farm. Harriet commented, "We are all very much pleased to hear it but Should like it better if we was all there" (August 31, 1854). Allen returned to Plymouth in September and auctioned off the household possessions the family would not need in the Midwest. On September 25, 1854, the family left New England, traveling west by train and arriving in Chicago on September 28. "We arrived here at 2 oclock almost tired out. In the morning Mr. H took his horse [and] went with us to our new home. The people have not moved out" (September 20, 1854).

The weeks that followed were filled with the details of establishing the new farm in Lyndon, Cook County, and Harriet recorded that Allen purchased two cows on October 16: "We was all very glad of them for we want the milk very much." Two days later she wrote, "Mr. Hemingway has been to work with his boys. He seems to enjoy it very much. I think we shall all enjoy our new home better when it comes warm wether. We are quite contented as we expected to be." A month later the children started school, studying with a Mr. Clark, who boarded with the Hemingways for a time. On Sundays the schoolhouse served as the Methodist Church. Despite their status as newcomers, Allen was elected president of the Bible Meeting on December 30, 1854.

The years that followed reflect the normal family triumphs and tragedies of the age, and Harriet's diaries contain accounts of daily activities, family landmarks, and occasional glimpses into the values and assumptions of the Illinois Hemingways. Harriet wrote much of love, love sacred, familial, and physical: "I feel as if I could not content myself without my husband" (January 6, 1855). Allen sold Seth Thomas clocks wholesale in Chicago, commuting on the train, and the boys, with their father's guidance, developed the farm, although Rodney seems for a time to have worked in Chicago. Harriet recorded the prices for potatoes and corn, wheat and wood, as well as events that changed the family: Mary Ann married George H. Stoughton on March 11, 1855; Allen's younger brother, Jacob, came to visit; and young Delly injured himself on June 24 and died a week later. Harriet responded to the death of her youngest child, not yet two years old, with the acceptance of the faithful: "Delly had a very poor night and is very low today. Dr. called this morning. He spoke very encouraging about him but about 12 oclock he began to fail and died at 1" (July 31). She tempered her laments with the consolation of celestial purpose: "He was buried at 10 oclock this morning in our lot a few rods west of the house. I feel very lonely without him. It was very hard to part with him. The Lord has a right to his own" (August 1). On August 12 she reflected, "It is very lonely without Delly. He was a great deal of company for us. I miss him very much but all is for the best." Harriet would need the comforts of her faith in the years ahead.

By 1856 the family settled into a pattern. Allen and Rodney worked in Chicago during the week and farmed on weekends, aided by George and, increasingly, young Anson. They remained active in the church, concerned about the education of their children, and developed the farm to the point that Allen sold his clock business in late 1856. That left the parents free the following fall, after harvest, to travel to Arkansas to visit Harriet's brother, Willys Tyler, a blacksmith. They took a train to Cairo, Illinois, boarded the steamboat *Montgomery* for Napoleon, Ohio, and arrived in Memphis the next day. When the Hemingways reached the Arkansas River, they changed steamboats for the journey to Little Rock, then Fort Smith, and finally to Brown's Landing. There was nothing particularly remarkable about the journey except the fact that Anson would travel almost precisely the same route six years later during the Civil War.

The war brought more tragedy for the Hemingway family than they could have imagined when they moved west. It was not at all unusual that the regiment the youngest Hemingway boys joined was a volunteer military organization sponsored by the local Board of Trade. When word of the firing on Fort Sumter reached Illinois on April 15, 1861, Governor Richard Yates called for an immediate volunteer force of 6,000 men.[4] Within five days the state had exceeded its quota, and this tradition of stalwart patriotism continued to such an extent that it was not necessary to institute the federal conscription law enacted on March 3, 1863. Mustering rallies were held in virtually every community, and local governments offered bonuses for enlistment. There were also units organized and sponsored by private groups, and the State Agricultural Society furnished an entire brigade. Other military groups were formed by railroad workers, by the faculty and students of Illinois State Normal University, and by various nationalities, so that there were regiments comprised entirely of German, Irish, Scottish, Portuguese, and Jewish soldiers. A Congregational pastor, the Reverend B. C. Ward, put together a company made up entirely of ministers who were not to serve as chaplains but to "stand up for Christ on the field of battle." By the end of the war, Illinois had contributed more than 250,000 Union soldiers. Almost 30,000 Illinois men died during the conflict, nearly two-thirds of them from disease rather than wounds.[5]

When the Civil War erupted, the Hemingway boys joined volunteer Illinois outfits. George went first, serving in the Eighteenth Illinois Infantry with a close friend of the family, Will Holton. Rodney and Anson, only seventeen, joined later, when the Chicago Board of Trade organized a regiment. Only Anson survived. Young Holton fell at the battle of Chattanooga; George died in a hospital in Cairo, Illinois, on October 18, 1862. Anson did not learn of the death of his brother until his father came down river to tell him. Anson's diary entry for October 21, 1862, says cryptically that his father brought the news that George was dead, that he had died in Cairo from dysentery, and that father was going to take him home. Rodney died six months later in a hospital in Memphis, Tennessee. Anson, often ill and exhausted, served for two years, primarily on guard duty, and was discharged on March 30, 1864, to receive a commission in Natchez as a first lieutenant in the Seventieth U.S. Colored Infantry. When the war ended, he stayed in the South, serving as the acting Provost Marshal of the Freedman's Bureau in Natchez and primarily arranging contracts for freed slaves to work for plantation owners. Anson returned home in 1866 and enrolled at the academy of Wheaton College, determined, at age twenty-two, to finish his high school education. One evening soon after he arrived he attended a prayer meeting at which he was introduced to Adelaide Edmonds, whom he married on August 17, 1867.

Anson and Adelaide lived on the corner of Tyler and Paulina Streets in Chicago during the decade he served as General Secretary of the Chicago YMCA, which he had founded, and both were active in the Union Park Congregational Church. Their first child, Anginette, was born in Chicago in 1869, just before they moved to Oak Park, settling in a house on the corner of Oak Park Avenue and Superior Street. Here he founded the real estate business in the village he was to call home for 58 years, and here Clarence Edmonds Hemingway (Ernest Hemingway's father) was born on September 4, 1871, followed by Willoughby in 1874 (picking up the name of Anson's brother Willis), George in 1876 (named after the brother who died in the war), Alfred in 1877, and Grace in 1881.[6] But even in suburban Chicago the Hemingways were never far from agrarian life: during Clarence's teenage years he was sent out to work on his grandfather's farm, for Allen survived until 1886. And Clarence, in turn, put his oldest son, Ernest, to work on Longfield Farm in Michigan, across Walloon Lake from Windemere. The assumption of the age, one lost in modern times, was that there was dignity in manual labor and moral instruction in working close to the soil.

Clarence graduated from Oak Park High School in 1890, spent three years in a premed program at Oberlin College,[7] completed his medical training at Rush Medical College, and returned to Oak Park to practice. There he married Grace Hall of Oak Park on October 1, 1896, and there they had six children, beginning with Marcelline in 1898 and Ernest a year later. The children inherited intelligence and talent and a penchant for science from the Hemingway side and for art from their mother. Theirs was a fascinating household, filled with devotion to family and religion, with music and adventure and family lore, and the lives of the children would be enriched by it.

In 1899, Oak Park was a country village with unpaved streets and no electricity.[8] Dr. Hemingway used a horse and buggy to make his housecalls, and he did not buy an automobile until 1911. The Civil War veterans, Anson Hemingway among them, were still local heroes, and everyone voted Republican, remembering that the Democratic Party had supported slavery and opposed the war. The town was a bastion of midwestern values, believing in devotion to family and community, progressive Protestantism, rugged individualism, and limited government. There were no income taxes, no saloons, and virtually no crime. Local citizens took pride in the past and distrusted the future, especially the new liberties and wild music favored by the younger generation. In many ways the Hemingways were among the progressives. Following his father's dedication to organizations for young boys, Dr. Hemingway founded the Agassiz Club, an organization dedicated to the moral instruction of young boys. Grace Hall Hemingway, encouraged by her parents, was active in the push for women's suffrage, and she rejected traditional assumptions about gender roles. As Ernest's brother, Leicester, observed, his mother "lacked domestic talents," and she concerned herself with music and art and left household tasks to others. The Hemingway family was much present in the community, with Anson the head of a real estate firm and a frequent speaker at civic and church events. Adelaide remained the matriarch of the family, active in community service organizations. George was in business with Anson, and Clarence (called "Ed" locally) was attaining prominence as the village obstetrician. Willoughby was also a physician, but he was serving as a missionary in China and was much revered as an emblem of Oak Park's service to the world. The name "Hemingway" meant something in the village in those days, and, prior to World War I, Ernest was certainly not the most notable member of the family.

Indeed, as his high school contemporaries recalled in 1973, Ernie Hemingway was a very ordinary member of the class of 1917, not the most popular of young men (no one could remember his having had a date), not an outstanding student (nearly the entire class, other than Ernest, went on to college), hardly an athletic hero of any kind, with work on the school newspaper and literary magazine as his most notable accomplishments.[9] In retrospect, these early literary efforts, now brought together in a volume entitled *Hemingway at Oak Park High School,* constitute a considerable body of work that anticipates in significant ways the celebrated fiction in the 1920s, but young Ernest's efforts as a writer were regarded at the time as well within the "normal" range of talent and intelligence. It was not until his service in the American Red Cross in Italy in World War I, when he was wounded on the front lines in July 1918, that Hemingway gained heroic stature.[10] The local newspaper, *Oak Leaves,* ran a front-page story of his wounding and followed it with his letters to his family, reports of the medals he had received, and comments from people who had known him. When he returned home early in 1919, his appearances at the high school produced a sensation, with Hemingway displaying the blood-stained uniform in which he was wounded and relating fanciful tales of the heroic exploits of the Italian Arditi. In response the student body rose and sang a song they had memorized:

> Hemingway, we hail you the victor,
> Hemingway, ever winning the game,
> Hemingway, you've carried the colors
> For our land you've won fame.
> Hemingway, we hail you the leader,
> Your deeds—every one shows your valor.
> Hemingway, Hemingway, you've won
> —Hemingway![11]

The rest of the spring was essentially a period of convalescence for Ernest, who was recovering from the shrapnel and machine gun wounds he had sustained in the war and from the rejection of Agnes von Kurowsky, a Red Cross nurse he courted in Milan during his hospitalization.[12] It was his last prolonged period in Oak Park.

By May, Hemingway had recovered sufficiently to move to Walloon Lake for the summer, and he stayed on into the fall, working, with mixed results, on such early stories as "The Woppian Way" and "The Mercenaries." He returned to Oak Park for Christmas that year, but in January 1920 he took a position in Toronto as a companion to Ralph Connable, a young man who had been disabled from birth.[13] Hemingway also began publishing freelance stories for the *Toronto Star*. He stopped briefly in Oak Park in the late spring of 1920 and spent the early part of the summer at Walloon Lake until his birthday on July 21, when his mother insisted that he leave the residence, incensed at his idleness and insensitivity in getting his younger sisters and their friends involved in a drinking party.[14] After an interval in Petosky, a small Michigan town near Walloon Lake, Ernest moved to Chicago, taking an editorship on the *Cooperative Commonwealth* magazine, and he still held this position when he married Hadley Richardson in September 1921. In December they left the United States for Paris, and he never again lived for any extended period in Oak Park or the Chicago area.

This was the decade of American expatriatism, and it was not remarkable that an aspiring young writer should go to Paris for his apprenticeship. Ernest had seen the city on his way to Italy in 1918, the living was easy and inexpensive, and the Left Bank was quickly becoming a haven for American writers and artists impatient with middle-class morality in the United States. As he was well aware, Paris was also very much part of Hemingway family lore: maternal grandfather Ernest Hall had visited there in 1875 as part of his grand tour; paternal grandfather Anson Hemingway had spent several months in Europe, including Paris, in 1881. In the next generation, both of Hemingway's parents spent time in Paris. In July of 1895, after a sojourn in Great Britain, visiting poor children in Scotland as part of his philanthropic work, Clarence went on to Paris in August, stopping at the Hotel Regent at 16, Rue de Trévise. He had spent two weeks in Holland, Belgium, Prussia, Switzerland, and France, enjoying Versailles, relaxing for a time in Paris, and hearing *Otello* and *Lohengrin* at the Grand Opera. In an August 16, 1895, letter to Grace, he was pleased to report that "I am really getting so I can talk about Napoleon I, II and III and all the Louis's and Jean de Arc." Reflecting on his travels, he observed that "it has widened my ideas of real foreign travel wonderfully, for the striking contrast of the slow and contented Hollander with his wooden shoes, canals, and windmills to be compared with the twinkling eyed, flashy, treacherous wine soaked Frenchman. . . . " His son would develop a more positive attitude toward the French.

For her part, Grace spent time in Europe with her father after her months in New York taking voice lessons from Madame Cappriani, spending time at the Art Student's League, and learning to smoke. She sailed from New York on April 25, 1896, on the *R. M. S. Campania,* and wrote to Clarence that she was flirting outrageously "with any person of the male persuasion" but sharing sweet memories of something that had taken place on a *"tender sweet old red sofa,"* something unstated but obviously sexual and delightful that had bound the two of them together forever. She landed on May 2 in Bath, too ill to enjoy herself, but within five days she was on her way to Barnstable and London. By May 20 she was in Paris, staying at her "old stamping ground" (clearly suggesting that she had been there before), the Hotel Burgundy, at 8, Rue Duphot. In the week that followed she explored the Louvre, much more a student of art than her son would ever become, and took carriage rides down the Champs-Elysées to the Arc de Triomphe and back to the hotel by way of the Madelaine. She attended mass at Notre Dame, dined at the boulevard cafés, strolled in the Jardin du Luxembourg, and examined the gallery, especially the exhibit of modern art. She, too, made the trip to Versailles, marveled at the Eiffel Tower, and wept when she heard *Faust* at the Grand Opera. Returning to London, she saw *Lohengrin* at Covent Garden, soaked for two weeks at

Bath, and sailed for America from Liverpool to prepare for her wedding. Although his parents did not live in Paris for as long as Ernest did, his descriptions of life there would have called up old memories for them, not the innocent imaginings of land-bound Oak Parkers in awe of the worldly sophistication of their adventuresome son.

Even in Paris, Ernest was never far from Oak Park, and he returned to his origins for the most important of his early stories, writing about life in Michigan, about the tension between his parents, about the shock of war and the disillusionment of returning home to a world that did not understand what had happened to him. What is most remarkable is that he never wrote a story set specifically in Oak Park, never used the details of his youth to portray the life he had known, never represented his childhood friends and his neighborhood in his early work. Even more astonishing, however, is that despite over a hundred scholarly books on Hemingway's life and work, there has never before been one dedicated to an examination of his life in Oak Park and the influence it had on his fiction. That is the subject of the essays collected in this volume, new scholarly examinations from a variety of perspectives, all attempting to come to terms with the Oak Park legacy and its impact on the formative years of Hemingway's career.

In "High Culture and Low: Hemingway's Oak Park before the Great War," Michael Reynolds sketches a detailed portrait of Hemingway's parents in the early years of their marriage as well as of the Oak Park of Hemingway's youth. He explains the nature of the high school Hemingway attended and of Hemingway's later comments about Oak Park. In "Hemingway's Religious Odyssey: The Oak Park Years," Larry E. Grimes explores the religious climate of Oak Park during Ernest's childhood, particularly with regard to the theological posture of the Reverend William E. Barton of the First Congregational Church. With unique insight into the religious context of the day, Grimes outlines the central issues of religious concern during Hemingway's formative years and the ways in which those issues are exhibited in his early fiction.

In "*John Halifax, Gentleman* and the Literary Courtship of Clarence and Grace," James Nagel uses the love letters of Hemingway's parents to demonstrate that their courtship and view of the world were profoundly influenced by their reading of American and British literature, especially Miss Mulock's popular Victorian novel *John Halifax, Gentleman*. When they were apart during much of 1895, the two young lovers arranged to read the same chapters of the novel at the same time, communicating through the romantic ideals of literature their most profound hopes for the future. It is not insignificant that they named their daughter "Ursula" after the heroine of this novel, and Grace took the name "Longfield Farm" from this book for her property across Walloon Lake.

David Marut, in "Out of the Wastebasket: Hemingway's High School Stories," provides a detailed consideration of "The Judgment of Manitou," "A Matter of Colour," and "Septi Jingan," all written while Hemingway was still in high school. Marut shows that many of Hemingway's characteristic elements of method and subject were present even in these juvenile stories, long before he became friends with Sherwood Anderson, Gertrude Stein, and other established writers of the day. It is clear from these works that Hemingway, as a student in high school, was already writing about the betrayal of friendship and its disillusionment, the trauma of violence and its psychological effect, and that his characters were boxers, Native Americans, and woodsmen confronting the cruel realities of an indifferent nature. These realizations, along with Marut's sensitive observations about the fictional methods of these early stories, make them essential for a full understanding of the development of Hemingway's fundamental style and narrative strategies.

In "Oak Park as the Thing Left Out: Surface and Depth in 'Soldier's Home,' " Carlos Azevedo employs a biocritical approach to analyze not only the dynamic between Krebs and his mother in the story but the biographical resonance of the events as well. Azevedo perceives Grace Hall Hemingway as the embodiment of the narrow values of Oak Park in the early century, with its emphasis on religious creeds and a middle-class work ethic, and he maintains that Ernest's break from his mother contained complex depths of feeling on all levels, including sexual, that provided an undercurrent for the fiction he wrote years later. Turning to the story itself, Azevedo explores the text in terms of these issues, paying close attention to the mother-son conflict at the heart of the tale and the submerged sister-brother attraction.

In "Romantic Betrayal in 'Ten Indians,' " Mary Anne O'Neal explores not only the theme of romantic disillusionment but also the destruction of the wilderness and the way of life of Native Americans. She outlines the biographical origins of Hemingway's use of Ojibway characters in his work and his utilization of such characters in his early "The Judgment of Manitou" and "Sepi Jingan" as well as in newly discovered manuscript fragments entitled "No Worse Than a Bad Cold" and "The Indians Moved Away." This background information informs and enlivens her explication of the central themes of "Ten Indians" and supports her conclusion that the story is crucial to the Nick Adams sequence in capturing the moment of initiation into some of the painful realities of the adult world while commemorating the lost world of the wilderness and the Indian way of life.

In "Women in the Garden: Hemingway's 'Summer People' and 'The Last Good Country,' " Abby H. P. Werlock focuses on gender issues in two posthumous stories discovered by Philip Young in 1967. After establishing a biographical foundation in Hemingway's youthful experiences in northern Michigan, the setting for both of these stories, and explaining the direct correspondences between actual people and the characters in these works, she examines gender and sexuality. In the process she touches on not simply "sex" but the more complicated matters of androgyny, sexual exchange, male bonding, incest, and forbidden love that are submerged in these works, in the process suggesting that may be why they were never published during Hemingway's lifetime.

George Monteiro reaches back to Izaak Walton's *The Compleat Angler* to challenge the widely held assumption that the central activity in "Big Two-Hearted River" is the ritualistic healing of the effects of Nick's wounding in World War I, an interpretation made popular in the scholarship of Philip Young. Monteiro argues that the story is a superb rendering of the art of fishing that rivals the original georgic on the subject by Walton. To buttress this reading, Monteiro goes back to Hemingway's youthful articles in the *Toronto Star* and his description of fishing in his other works, most notably *To Have and Have Not, The Old Man and the Sea, Islands in the Stream,* and *The Garden of Eden.* Out of this contemplation comes not only a new reading but a new historical context in which to understand what Hemingway was doing in the concluding story of his first important collection, *In Our Time.*

Judy Hen provides a unique approach to Hemingway's first novel, *The Sun Also Rises,* by focusing on the ethic of work in the life of Jake Barnes and his circle of friends. Hen explores the idea of employment in the Hemingway family and the life of Oak Park as well as the expanded concept of work that includes sports and leisure activities as well. She also discusses the concept in Hemingway's letters and essays in the early 1920s, which reveal his commitment to the traditional Protestant work ethic. From this perspective, she formulates a new and challenging interpretation of Hemingway's novel of the lost generation.

The concluding essay in the collection, John J. Fenstermaker's "The Search for an American Audience: Marketing Ernest Hemingway, 1925–1930," shifts the attention beyond Hemingway's literary apprenticeship and into the beginnings of his fame as an important author. Focusing on Hemingway's early relationships with his publishers, particularly Boni and Liveright and then Charles Scribner's Sons, Fenstermaker traces their attempts to market their young author and introduce him to the world, attempts that proved successful but were not without elements of humor, excess, and ineptitude. Fenstermaker concludes his study with the promotion and success of three of the early books, *The Sun Also Rises, Men Without Women,* and *A Farewell to Arms.* In the process he charts how Hemingway became a world-famous writer and how that fame changed the course of modern literature.

The afterword by Morris Buske, a revered former history teacher at Oak Park and River Forest High School and a founding member of The Ernest Hemingway Foundation of Oak Park, provides a valuable study in contrast between Hemingway's two grandfathers, Ernest Hall and Anson Hemingway, and the differing values of the two families, who lived across the street from one another. With unique information and perception, Buske outlines the underlying doctrine in each of the families, the artistic Hall home, where Ernest was born and lived for his first six years, and the more rational and scientific home of Anson Hemingway, who provided a model for Ernest's later experiences in war.

No members of the Hemingway family still live in Oak Park, but the family is very much there. The house in which Ernest was born is now a historical building owned and operated by The Ernest Hemingway Foundation of Oak Park; just down the street is the Hemingway museum, an archive with family birth certificates, wills, marriage licenses, divorce papers, military records, photographs, and hundreds of letters. Thousands of visitors drift through the museum every year, searching for some insight into the creative energy and sensibility that accounts for Hemingway's astonishing production. A few blocks away, on Kenilworth Avenue, rests the house the Hemingways occupied during Ernest's adolescence, and near that home is the Oak Park and River Forest High School, where Fannie Biggs and Margaret Dixon taught Ernest literature in the Oxford Room, now the focus of local tours. Every summer Oak Park celebrates Hemingway Days with a mock running of the bulls, concerts, a picnic in the town park, and discussions and lectures about the favorite son. Throughout his life, wherever he went, Oak Park was always in Ernest Hemingway, in his politics, his worldview, his sense of himself, his literary sensibility. And now, three decades after his death, he is always in Oak Park, in its pride as a community, in the promise it holds for its children, in its streets and schools and sense of itself. Ernest Hemingway, Nobel Prize Laureate for Literature, citizen of the world and one of the most famous persons in it, is still present in the place of his beginnings, in the village on the prairie he never really left.

NOTES

1. Throughout her diary, Harriet invariably spells the name of her second son as "Willys," although Patricia S. Hemingway gives the name as "Willis." See Patricia S. Hemingway, *The Hemingways: Past and Present and Allied Families* (Baltimore: Gateway Press, Inc., 1988), 153. This volume, which is the source of a good deal of my information on the Hemingway family, is hereafter cited as *The Hemingways*. I am indebted to Doris Hemingway for permission to quote from documents in her private collection, especially the diary of Harriet Hemingway and the letters of Grace and Clarence Hemingway. The Sanford family and the Illinois State Archives graciously provided access to the Civil War diaries of Anson Hemingway.

2. Harriet here wrote "to the" when she clearly meant "the."

3. These entries must have interested Anson decades later, when he read his mother's diaries; he wrote notes next to significant events, paying particular attention to the age of his parents.

4. For the historical context of volunteer enlistment in Illinois, see Arthur Charles Cole, *The Era of the Civil War, 1848–1870* (Springfield: Illinois Centennial Commission, 1919), 273–88.

5. Cole, *Era of the Civil War*, 280, 284.

6. The fact that there was already a Grace Hemingway accounts for the fact that when Clarence married Grace Hall she used the name "Grace Hall Hemingway."

7. Clarence did not receive a degree from Oberlin College, as has been widely reported. An excellent student, he left on schedule to enter medical school.

8. The best source for Oak Park and the Hemingway family is "Time Was," the first chapter of Michael Reynolds, *The Young Hemingway* (New York: Basil Blackwell, 1986), 1–15. I am indebted to this book and to many conversations with Reynolds for my insights into the community.

9. See Ina Mae Schleden and Marion Rawls Herzog, eds., *Ernest Hemingway as Recalled by His High School Contemporaries* (Oak Park, Ill.: The Historical Society of Oak Park and River Forest, 1973). For more information about the high school, see *Oak Park and River Forest High School: 1873–1976* (Oak Park, Ill.: Osla Graphics, n.d.).

10. Hemingway's exploits in World War I have been widely examined both for biographical interests and as the background for *The Sun Also Rises, A Farewell to Arms*, and a number of important stories, among them "In Another Country," "Now I Lay Me," and "A Way You'll Never Be." See, for example, Michael S. Reynolds, *Hemingway's First War: The Making of A Farewell to Arms* (Princeton: Princeton University Press, 1976) and Henry S. Villard and James Nagel, *Hemingway in Love and War: The Lost Diary of Agnes von Kurowsky* (Boston: Northeastern University Press, 1989).

11. See Cynthia Maziarka and Donald Vogel, Jr., eds., *Hemingway at Oak Park High* (Oak Park: Oak Park and River Forest High School, 1993), 117–23.

12. For a detailed discussion of both the wounding and the romance, see Nagel, "Hemingway and the Italian Legacy," *Hemingway in Love and War*, 197–269.

13. See Carlos Baker, *Ernest Hemingway: A Life Story* (New York: Scribners, 1969), 66–67.

14. Max Westbrook, "Grace under Pressure: Hemingway and the Summer of 1920," in *Ernest Hemingway: The Writer in Context*, ed. James Nagel (Madison: University of Wisconsin Press, 1984), 77–106.

Hemingway:
The Oak Park
Background

MICHAEL REYNOLDS

High Culture and Low:
Oak Park before the Great War

THE OAK PARK that nurtured young Ernest Hemingway and the music that once played there can never be completely recovered, for the metaphoric distances, as Hemingway might say, have all changed. What scholars unearth from old newspapers, unreferenced letters, and curious photographs is never the village itself, never the times or the people. The Oak Park air no longer smells as it once did in autumns of burning leaves; the horse barns and livery stables have crumbled to dust. The collective village memory is selective and seldom verifiable, and out of memory, dead documents, and fading gravestones we reconstruct the past to suit our present needs. What we think happened, did happen, as long as we believe in it.

Hemingway's high school classmates remembered young Ernest for his spirit and humor, if not his manners. Sue Lowrey Kesler said that Ernie was "always laughing, carefree; rather tousled and unkempt as to appearance."[1] Other girls in his class were more blunt. One said, "Confidentially, he was not too popular and none of 'us girls' dated him."[2] Another said, "He did not care too much what his classmates thought of his personal appearance. . . . Ernie was a handsome boy . . . but he did not care how he looked. Unkempt is the only word to describe him."[3] Grace Knold Gjesdahl thought young Hemingway's "aloofness and his conceit . . . did not make for close associations. . . . We wished he would pay a little more attention to the back of his neck and his finger nails!"[4]

Compared to adolescents today, Ernest appears terribly respectable in photographs, but his classmates remembered his appearance as evidence of his rebellion against Oak Park and family norms. Carol Derenforth Lowitz said that he "would almost refuse to conform to the standard of ethics set up by his class mates," an attitude that she attributed to his reaction against his "pedantic and straight-laced family."[5] The doctor and the doctor's wife, Grace Hall Hemingway, were never pedantic, and "straight-laced" does not describe Grace's own rebellion against Oak Park restrictions.

Ernest's classmates never saw his high school notebooks, where he began his lifelong obsession with lists and promises. On those private pages, he inventoried himself and his dreams. His list of possessions included two suits (one worn out and one good), six shirts, three pairs of shoes, magazines and books, a rifle, a shotgun and a box of shells, fishing hooks, line, flies, a baseball bat and glove, two account books, a "chronic case of piles" and "a lot of knowledge about woodcraft, hunting, fishing . . . farming, lumbering, etc."[6] The list was dated March 21, 1915. Ernest Hemingway was fifteen years old on that spring solstice, and this was no casual list, but an accounting as focused as Thoreau's inventory of his costs at Walden.

On the same day, Hemingway mapped out his future:

I desire to do pioneering or exploring work in the 3 last great frontiers[:] Africa[,] southern central South America[,] or the country around and north of Hudson Bay. I believe that the Science, English and to a certain extent the Latin that I am now studying in highschool will help me in this object. I intend to specialize in the sciences in college and to join some expedition when I leave college. I believe that any training I get by hiking in the spring or farm work in the summer or any work in the woods which tends to develop resourcefulness and self reliance is of inestimable value in the work I intend to pursue.

I have no desire absolutely to be a millionaire or a rich man
but I do intend to do something toward the scientific interests of
the world.[7]

He read it over, and then he signed it: Ernest M. Hemingway, a
binding contract with himself made on that first day of spring, a
contract he kept with the world as well as he was able.

He never enrolled at college, but he never gave up his studies
in natural history, ichthyology, or unencumbered spaces. His language studies broadened: Italian, French, Spanish, and a smat-
tering of German. He never got to Hudson Bay or South America, but he took us with him to Africa. He studied trout streams
in several countries, studied Gulf Stream marlin, studied Spanish
bulls and African game. He studied the flight of birds, the bends
of rivers, and the flow of country. But what he studied first, last,
and always was that strange animal, humanity, rampant in its
natural setting. Like his mother, Ernest was an artist; like his
father, he was a natural historian; like both, he found his calling
in Oak Park. But like neither parent, he was a child of this century, born too late for the frontier and too soon for outer space,
leaving him only the dark country within himself to explore.

Remembering right, as Gertrude Stein said, is never easy and
seldom achieved. All people have their own stories. When Malcolm Cowley began his 1948 *Life* magazine feature on Hemingway, he relied on his Oak Park informant, Otto McFeely, the editor of *Oak Leaves,* who passed along hearsay and interviewed
some Hemingway classmates for their memories. Phil White's response is representative of McFeely's information. White said:

I was smaller than he [Hemingway] was, but I could always lick
him when we were grade school boys and I know as old as I am,
I could lick him today. He always was yellow. He always tried to
be the big shot and never was. He never dated girls or went to
dancing school until he was in the last year of high school when
he seemed to get an idea of what girls were for. It is said that in
his last year he had a very ardent and successful affair with a
high school teacher who was then thirty years old.[8]

25

That Hemingway actually began dance classes, along with most of his peers, in the fall of his sophomore year, that he dated Dorothy Davies and Frances Coates in his junior year, or took Jean Pickett and Katherine Bagley canoeing while making a play for Annette, had dropped from White's memory.[9] It is also unlikely that Hemingway had an affair with his senior English teacher, Fannie Biggs, although he must have found her attractive, for there is a strong resemblance between Biggs and Hemingway's first wife, Hadley Richardson. As with many memoirs, White's tells more about Oak Park's response to the adult Hemingway than it does about Ernest's early life in Oak Park.

The Oak Park of Hemingway's youth, which has eroded beneath the pressures of this century, was a moral outpost from Chicago, "the city on the hill" that voted Republican at every chance. In the Bull Moose election of 1912, half of the male population cast votes, sixty percent of them for Roosevelt.[10] With its insistence on moral behavior, parental control, and constant vigil against corrupting forces, Oak Park put a good deal of pressure on its sons and daughters. That some, like Hemingway, seemed to rebel against those pressures is not surprising; in fact, had that first generation of this century not rebelled, it would have been strange indeed. In the Oak Park of his youth, Hemingway was theoretically protected by city ordinances from uncensored movies, boxing matches, any information on venereal disease or birth control, all forms of gambling and prostitution, and all consumption of alcohol. Until he turned eighteen, Hemingway could not legally buy cigarettes, play billiards, drive a car, or own a cap gun within the village limits. Unless accompanied by a parent or responsible adult, Hemingway had an eight P.M. curfew in the fall and winter, nine P.M. in spring and summer.[11]

Not too surprisingly, Ernest, like more than one of his classmates, became fascinated with drinking, gambling, and prizefights, for whatever knowledge is forbidden to children becomes the coin of their realm. In Oak Park or, more likely, across the boulevard in Cicero, he took his first illegal drink and learned the fine art of rolling dice, "galloping dominoes" as he called it. He engaged in sponsored activities that got him out of the house after curfew: high school sports, the YMCA, the school orchestra. One day he shot a pheasant on Wallace Evans's game farm, violating Oak Park ordinances against carrying weapons and being out after curfew, not to mention stealing.[12] That readers have taken such rebellion as Hemingway's rejection of Oak Park is unfortunate. One may rage against one's cultural inheritance but can no more reject it than one's blood type.

Although Hemingway was sometimes embarrassed by his mother's free spirit and frightened by his father's retreat into depression, Hemingway's early years were not scarred by divorce or abuse; he grew up respecting his elders, submitting to discipline, and behaving like a good bad boy. In the protective village it was easy to be bad and just as easy to be forgiven, for the Hemingway name was a substantial one within the community. As Zelma Morton remembered, "If Ernest was not really popular neither did any Oak Parker ever ignore a Hemingway."[13] His extended family, largely educated at Wheaton College, Oberlin College, and Rush Medical School, was well known and well liked; his grandfather, Anson, uncle, Willoughby, and parents were all featured at various times on the cover of *Oak Leaves*. His father was a professional, his mother classically trained in music. They lived in a respectable neighborhood of businessmen, salesmen, doctors, and dentists, most of whom took the train each morning into Chicago, where they worked.[14] Although not as fine as John Farson's Pleasant Home, there was nothing shabby about the three-story Hemingway house, with its seven bedrooms, two full baths and two half baths, a large music studio, a living room of comparable size, a dining room and kitchen, Dr. Hemingway's office, and a large screened porch.[15]

There was also nothing shabby about the music that drenched Hemingway during his early years. Otto McFeely, remembering Grace Hall Hemingway long after her musical prime, saw her as "a frequent figure at art teas, weddings of scions of old families and at the Nineteenth Century Club, [she] wore long skirts before the New Look and always recalled to me the . . . Dowager Queen of England who also is very unfashionable. . . . Like most persons with the artistic flair, especially those who suffer the disaster of a little talent, she was also a 'character' who often caused people to smile, but always indulgently."[16] Hemingway himself further obscured his mother's personality when he professed to hate her and when he later held her responsible for his father's suicide. It became convenient for Hemingway to blame his mother for problems he did not want to face.

When Grace Hall Hemingway designed their Kenilworth house, she included a music studio and recital hall thirty feet square with a vaulted ceiling and a narrow balcony. Here she gave music and voice lessons, scheduled her student recitals, and composed and practiced her own music, which was marketed by two different publishing houses. Today her lyrics, mostly written for contraltos like herself, are as dated as the long Victorian dresses she wore until her death in 1951, but they are no more sentimental than most turn-of-the-century popular music.[17] Among her publications are such titles as "If I Could Know," "I'll Sing the Songs of Araby," "God Laid Me Aside to Rest Me," "For You and Me," "Starlight Serenade," and "The Sweetest Song I Know."[18] Ernest must have known by heart her "Flower Lullaby," with cello obbligato:

> Hush, hush
> My heart is singing low
> While rocking to and fro
> Lullaby, lullaby
> Sleep, darling child
> Dream of angel faces
> That loved thee long ago
> Dream of soft, sweet kisses
> That mother's lips bestow
> Hush Hush.[19]

However sweet and sometimes cloying Grace's lyrics might sound today, her music remains as demanding as when first written. With her large hands, she used chords stretching a full octave; in some cases, the harmony was played in the treble while the bass carried the melody. "If I Could Know" is not a beginner's piece, written with six flats.

No matter how egocentric a mother or how curious a personality Grace Hall Hemingway may seem today, it is a mistake to think of her as a pushy amateur musician whom Oak Park tolerated with amusement. In a village filled with amateurs, Grace was a professional musician whose classically trained skills became her identity and her freedom. Wherever one went in Oak Park, Grace was singing by invitation. At the Third Congregational Church she chaired the music committee and directed fifty children in the vested choir and orchestra.[20] When the Women's Christian Temperance Union met to reaffirm Oak Park's dry status, Grace "added to the pleasure of those present by singing a solo."[21] When the Three O'Clock Club met, "the attraction was Mrs. Grace Hall Hemingway in one of her charming and versatile programs."[22] Two weeks later she entertained the Nineteenth Century Club with her Shakespearean song routine from *As You Like It*.[23] A month later she was entertaining the high school parent-teacher association with Irish ballads like "Mollie Bawn" and Longfellow's "Home Song."[24] On one of her almost annual trips to California, Grace was

> received with great enthusiasm in the professional musical circle
> of Los Angeles [where she sang] at a reception to the leading
> musical lights. . . . Later Mrs. Hemingway gave a recital at
> Blanchard Hall Building, assisted by Miss Henderson of the New
> York Castle Square Opera Company. . . . Last Friday evening Mrs.
> Hemingway was heard at The Abbotsford Inn, an invitation af-
> fair. Saturday afternoon she sang . . . for the musical critics of
> the press, and on Saturday evening gave a private recital of her
> own songs, with harp, violin, piano and pipe organ accompani-
> ment.[25]

Young Hemingway heard his mother practice her varied musical routines, her students at their lessons, and himself on his cello. He and his older sister, Marcelline, played in the high school student orchestra for two years. The impact of his musical training, both formal and casual, was long lasting. He listened to classical music throughout his life. During his courtship of Hadley Richardson, piano concerts were part of their shared interests; after their marriage, Hadley replaced his mother at the piano they rented in Paris. Out of this background came Hemingway's compulsion to public performance and his understanding of counterpoint, which he used to advantage in his writing.[26]

When his mother was not immersed in her music, she actively participated in the Nineteenth Century Club, Oak Park's continuing education for ladies of some leisure. Professors from the University of Chicago and national authorities lectured regularly on topics like Arthurian romance and the grail legends, Roman architecture, William James, women's suffrage, Ibsen's philosophy, and the causes of divorce. Added to the general meetings were the special sections devoted to music, art, literature, home management, education, social economics, and social reform, each with meetings and reports by the membership. Grace not only attended these events, taking notes, but she also contributed to them. Many of the subjects reinforced Ernest's high school course work and reading. The Humanities Research Center at the University of Texas houses Grace's elaborate notes on Aristophanes, Boccaccio, Euripides, Homer, and Greek music, drama, and poetry. One can also read her twenty-page manuscript "The Analogy between Music and Color" and her twenty-nine page manuscript on Russian music.[27] Given her gregarious nature, one can easily imagine that more than a little of her continuing education became a part of the Hemingways' household life, and much of her interests supplemented or reinforced her son's education.

At Oak Park and River Forest High School, Hemingway took the then standard precollege curriculum: six semesters of science, four of math, six of Latin, eight of English literature and composition, four of history, two of applied music, and two years of orchestra. In Latin, young Hemingway translated Cicero; in history he wrote essays on Greek tyrants and the Marathon campaign and outlined the Punic Wars. "It's a hard world," he wrote in the margin of his high school notebook, "and few of us get out of it alive."[28] His yearlong courses in American and ancient history were not grounded in the watered-down texts that are now written for high school students; Hemingway read and was tested on the standard histories of his day. His English courses required weekly writing and the study of composition, and Hemingway read the classic myths, Chaucer, Spenser, Shakespeare, Milton, Pope, the British romantics, Walter Scott, Dickens, George Eliot, Tennyson, Browning, and Matthew Arnold. He spent ten weeks studying the history of the English language, four weeks on formal rhetoric, and an entire semester of his senior year on prose composition.[29] Along with his classmates, Hemingway memorized the opening lines of Chaucer's general prologue to *The Canterbury Tales* and the then standard ration of Shakespeare soliloquies.[30] Whatever the course, humanities or science, there were always written assignments: weekly book reports, essays, and term papers. Hemingway outlined his reading of *Macbeth* and *Hamlet* and wrote reports on the anatomy of grasshoppers, the necessity of life insurance, the need for a standing army, and the causes of the American Revolution.[31]

He also wrote humorous pieces for the school newspaper and the literary magazine. John Gehlmann, one of Hemingway's English teachers, said, "I was always having to fight criticism by the superintendent (M. R. McDaniel) that Ernie was writing like Ring Lardner—and consequently a lost soul! Later Mr. McDaniel occasionally reminded me that Ernie got his start under me, and held me responsible for the malodorous writings from Ernie's pen."[32] In his high school translation of Cicero, Hemingway emphasized three lines that might well have been his motto during those years: "I pray Cataline to what point will you try our patience. How long will you still mock our rage. To what limit will you display your ungoverned insolence."[33]

The "Bill 3127 Introduced by Senator Hemingway" gives a quick impression of the high school humorist at work. It was

An act making policemen come under the Game Laws.

An act making it a misdemeanor to kill a policeman out of season.

An act providing that no policemen be killed during the mating season.

An act providing that no one person shall kill any more policemen in one day than he or his family can dispose of.

An act providing that a special license be issued to Taxidermists.

In his outline for library procedures, Hemingway included a list
of rules:

It is written that in the Library thou shalt not chew gum. Thou
shalt not covet thy neighbor's magazine orally. Thou shalt not
play tic tat-toe with Toots Johnson. Thou shalt not match pen-
nies with Reed Milliken. Thou shalt not throw paper wads with
Jim Adams. Neither shalt thou listen to Prieble and Worthington
tell the story of the fly in the hospital. Neither shalt thou read
the International Studio when studying the Ford Profit Sharing
Plan. . . . Thou shalt not kid the Jane that sitteth upon thy right
hand, nor kick the boob who sitteth across from thee. Thou shalt
not tip up the pollard ink well to see if it spilleth. It does.[34]

Most courses required collateral reading at both the high
school library and the Scoville Institute. Besides required texts,
Hemingway also found time to read the books he most enjoyed
at age sixteen, the short stories of O. Henry, Rudyard Kipling's
tales of empire, and Stewart Edward White's version of the stren-
uous life.[35] From the Scoville's collection, Hemingway borrowed
books, particularly during the summer, and he frequently had to
pay late fees.[36] Although he never went to college, in Oak Park
he acquired the cultural background he needed for the next step
in his life. By the time he was twenty-three, Hemingway was in
Paris reading Gertrude Stein, Ezra Pound, and James Joyce.

For the forty-two years of his life beyond the village, Hemingway left permanent records of his haunts and hideouts: Paris and
Pamplona, Key West and Cuba, Milan, Madrid, and the Seren-
geti. He wrote about every place he ever lived or spent significant
time except for Oak Park. Later, some would say he hated Oak
Park and its upper-middle-class hypocrisy, and there is some evidence to support this short-sighted view. When the Nineteenth
Century Club's book section brought in a Chicago critic to discuss Hemingway's first novel, *The Sun Also Rises,* his mother was

born of generic rebelliousness but precipitated by a midnight party on the beach, emphasizes the differences between his values and those of his parents, particularly as expressed in literature.[15] As Grace wrote to Clarence immediately after the incident, "Oh! but he is a cruel son. I got supper for him when he came home at 9 o'clock, last night, and sat down with him, for I had had none, and he insulted me every minute; said 'all I read was moron literature,' that Dr. Frank Crane who writes such glorious helpful articles in the *American* was the 'Moron's Maeterlinck' and asked me if I read the *Atlantic Monthly* just so some one would see me doing it. . . . He is distinctly a menace to youth."[16] It was inevitable that Hemingway's parents would find it difficult to accept the lifestyles, assumptions, and even language of their son's fiction, and their response to it must have been painful on both sides. As Marcelline remembered her father's reaction to *in our time*, "Daddy was so incensed that a son of his would so far forget his Christian training that he could use the subject matter and vulgar expressions this book contained that he wrapped and returned all six copies to the Three Mountains Press in Paris. He wrote to Ernest and told him that no gentleman spoke of venereal disease outside a doctor's office."[17] *The Sun Also Rises,* two years later, caused similar disruption despite the fact that it bears a formal resemblance to many aspects of *John Halifax.*

It should be said that there is no solid evidence that Ernest Hemingway ever read *John Halifax, Gentleman,* although it seems highly likely that his parents would have exposed him to it and to its underlying principles. The two books share some fascinating similarities. Both are retrospective, first-person novels, told by a maimed narrator who observes but cannot participate in courtship and who emphasizes the male friendships in his life. Both novels encapsulate the transitional ethics of an age, and both exalt a romantic pastoralism in contrast to the mercantile values of the city. *John Halifax* features a character named Jacob Baines, not far from Jacob Barnes but not close enough to demonstrate a direct borrowing. Another character in *John Halifax* roughly suggests Brett Ashley, for Lady Caroline is "designated from the first as a handsome, charming hedonist hell-bent on adultery,"[18] and, as does Lady Ashley, she escapes a husband in Britain for a liaison in Paris with her lover. What the narrator says of her could also stand for Brett: "Not that her conversation was brilliant or deep, but she said the most frivolous things in a way that made them appear witty; and the grand art, to charm by appearing charmed, was hers in perfection."[19] Ernest Hemingway had other sources for Brett and the events of *The Sun Also Rises,* people and events drawn from his own immediate experience, and it would not be responsible to conclude that *John Halifax* was the major influence on the events of the novel, although certain aspects of it may well have lingered in Hemingway's mind.

It does seem clear from the love letters of Clarence and Grace Hemingway that their romance was in many ways informed by their reading, and literature played an essential role in their sense of themselves and in their conduct as parents. From their books as well as from their own families, education, and religious training, they constructed a Victorian code of values that would guide them throughout their lives and that would eventually lead to a schism between them and their oldest son. Ernest's drinking, his divorce from Hadley, and his separation from the Congregational Church, all violations of his parents' creed, would have only exacerbated the break. But in a deeper sense it can also be said that to the extent that people never completely free themselves of the influence of their parents, even in their rebellion against them, one crucially important element in Ernest Hemingway's early life was the influence on his parents of Dinah Maria Craik's *John Halifax, Gentleman.*

NOTES

1. Mark Spilka, *Hemingway's Quarrel with Androgyny* (Lincoln: University of Nebraska Press, 1990), 18.

2. Carlos Baker, *Ernest Hemingway: A Life Story* (New York: Scribners, 1969), 567.

3. Spilka, *Hemingway's Quarrel,* 36.

4. I am grateful to Doris Hemingway for permission to quote from the letters in her possession. All correspondence between Clarence and

Grace Hemingway is from this collection, unless othewise noted, and will be identified by date within the text.

5. See James Lane Allen, *A Kentucky Cardinal: A Story* (New York: Harper, 1895).

6. William S. Ward, *A Literary History of Kentucky* (Knoxville: University of Tennessee Press, 1988), 42–43.

7. James Lane Allen, *Aftermath: Part Second of "A Kentucky Cardinal"* (New York: Harper, 1896).

8. Miss Mulock, [Dinah Maria Craik], *John Halifax, Gentleman* (New York: Thomas Y. Crowell, 1897). Clarence and Grace would not have read this edition, of course, but it is impossible to determine precisely which of the scores of editions they purchased.

9. Sally Mitchell, *Dinah Mulock Craik* (Boston: Twayne, 1983), 39.

10. Quoted in Mitchell, *Dinah Mulock Craik*, 51.

11. Spilka, *Hemingway's Quarrel*, 18.

12. Several Chicago editions were available by the 1890s, among them an undated one by the Union School Furnishing Company and another published by Belford in 1887. Clarence and Grace also had access to several editions published in New York, of course.

13. Marcelline Hemingway Sanford, *At the Hemingways: A Family Portrait* (Boston: Little, Brown, 1961), 107.

14. Robert K. Helmle, "Boyhood Recollections of Ernest Hemingway and His Father," *The Toe River Anthology* (1979): 83–94.

15. For an excellent discussion of this incident, see Max Westbrook, "Grace under Pressure: Hemingway and the Summer of 1920," in *Ernest Hemingway: The Writer in Context*, ed. James Nagel (Madison: University of Wisconsin Press, 1984), 77–106.

16. Quoted in Westbrook, "Grace under Pressure," 82.

17. Sanford, *At the Hemingways*, 218.

18. Spilka, *Hemingway's Quarrel*, 38.

19. Mulock, *John Halifax*, 204.

Dr. Clarence "Ed" Hemingway with his parents, Anson Tyler and Adelaide Hemingway. Published with the permission of The Ernest Hemingway Foundation of Oak Park.

The piercing eyes of Dr. Clarence Hemingway are notable in this portrait (1914). Trained at Oberlin College and Rush Medical School, he was a popular physician in Oak Park. Published with the permission of The Ernest Hemingway Foundation of Oak Park.

Grace Hemingway in a recital gown (1914). A talented soprano, she had studied voice in New York in 1895 and often performed in Oak Park. Published with the permission of The Ernest Hemingway Foundation of Oak Park.

Dr. and Mrs. Hemingway were married in the First Congregational Church of Oak Park on October 1, 1896. Ernest was baptized there in 1899 on their wedding anniversary. Published with the permission of The Oak Park Public Library.

The home of Ernest Hall at 439 North Oak Park Avenue. Ernest Hemingway was born on July 21, 1899, in his mother's second floor bedroom, just to the left of the round turret. Published with the permission of The Ernest Hemingway Foundation of Oak Park.

On his last visit to Windemere in 1904, Ernest Hall posed with his grandchildren, Ernest, Ursula, and Marcelline. Ever the English gentleman, Mr. Hall wore a coat and tie in the north woods. Published with the permission of The Ernest Hemingway Foundation of Oak Park.

Ernest's fascination with war probably began with stories told by his grandfather Anson Hemingway, a Civil War veteran. Young Ernest, with fife, posed with his grandfather before a Memorial Day parade. Published with the permission of the John F. Kennedy Library, Boston.

Ernest (left) and Marcelline in the front yard of the Ernest Hall home. The Anson Hemingway home is visible across the street (1903). Published with the permission of The Ernest Hemingway Foundation of Oak Park.

Ernest at age six, about the time of the death of Grandfather Hall. Published with the permission of The Ernest Hemingway Foundation of Oak Park.

Ernest's boyhood home at 600 N. Kenilworth Ave. Just above the children (Ernest on left) is the bay window of the library, which also was the waiting room for Dr. Hemingway's patients. Ernest read everything available, including his father's medical journals. His bedroom was in the third floor dormer. Published with the permission of The Ernest Hemingway Foundation of Oak Park.

Ernest (fourth row, second from right) took part in the children's choir of the Third Congregational Church, directed by his mother. Published with the permission of the John F. Kennedy Library, Boston.

Ernest and Marcelline attended Oliver Wendell Holmes elementary school, from second through eighth grade. Ernest's seventh grade teacher recalled that Mrs. Hemingway came to school to suggest that *The Call of the Wild* was too violent for seventh graders. Published with the permission of The Historical Society of Oak Park.

The Early Fiction
of Ernest Hemingway

DAVID MARUT

Out of the Wastebasket: Hemingway's High School Stories

ERNEST HEMINGWAY disdained attempts by scholars to unearth the fiction he wrote before the 1924 publication of *in our time*. In the early 1950s, while compiling a dissertation on Hemingway's literary apprenticeship, Charles Fenton discovered just how little the famous writer thought of efforts to publish his earliest manuscripts. Through a variety of methods, Hemingway repeatedly tried to discourage Fenton from reprinting the short stories he had written for the *Tabula*, the literary magazine of Oak Park and River Forest High School. In a letter dated October 9, 1952, Hemingway chastised Fenton and told him, "writing that I do not wish to publish, you have no right to publish. I would no more do a thing like that to you than I would cheat a man at cards or rifle through his desk or wastebasket or read his personal letters. I think you should make an examination of conscience before you keep on with something you have been warned to cease and desist on and which will lead you if not to jail at least into plenty of trouble."[1] In another correspondence, Hemingway more pointedly told Fenton, "Christ: The *Tabula*. You know the worst thing you can do to a writer is to dig out his worthless and childish stuff which he deliberately never allows to be collected or republished. It is like publishing the contents of a wastebasket."[2] Fenton eventually gave up trying to reprint the *Tabula* stories for *The Apprenticeship of Ernest Hemingway;* the stories did not appear in their

81

entirely until Constance Cappel Montgomery's *Hemingway in Michigan,* published five years after Hemingway's death. Despite Hemingway's protestations, his earliest works have gained historical significance because of who he became after he was a high school writer. The three *Tabula* short stories, "The Judgment of Manitou," "A Matter of Colour," and "Sepi Jingan," require further consideration because they provide a starting point for assessing Hemingway's literary craft.

While the short fiction Hemingway wrote during his junior and senior years understandably suffers in comparison to vintage Hemingway (he was, after all, seventeen years old when the last of the stories appeared), his work for the *Tabula* shows both an early aptitude for fiction and a strong desire to write. As Carlos Baker observed, "Whatever else might be said of Ernest's fiction at this period, most of it was tough-minded, firmly plotted, original, and astonishingly free of those ineptitudes common to high school writing."[3] Baker's assessment seems valid based on several common aspects of the works. First, the stories have relatively little of the intrusive authorial commentary that might mark a novice writer; the characters are allowed to speak for themselves through localized dialogue.[4] The high school stories also embrace the brevity and leanness that mark the prototypical Hemingway minimalism: the longest of the three stories, "Sepi Jingan," is less than 1,000 words. That this compact style emerged before Hemingway's newspaper days at the *Kansas City Star* and previous to his conversations with Gertrude Stein and Ezra Pound perhaps testifies to the demanding standards of his Oak Park English teachers, Fannie Biggs, Margaret Dixon, and Frank Platt. Finally, the central themes of the three stories anticipate some of Hemingway's later works that examine both the effects of violence on individuals and the justice meted out by a brutal world. As Montgomery points out, the three *Tabula* short stories not only show "that he had formed the basis of his style, even as a junior in high school . . . [but] had chosen the subject of violence and manliness before his World War I experiences."[5] Denying the effects of Hemingway's newspaper employment in Toronto and Kansas City, the dual trauma of World War I, and his life as an expatriate would be foolish, but the high school stories seem to indicate that Hemingway recognized some of the inherent strengths of his writing early on in his literary apprenticeship.

On the recommendation of one of his English teachers, Dixon, Hemingway submitted "The Judgment of Manitou" to the *Tabula* in February 1916. The editor of the magazine hardly endorsed the piece without reservation but understood that "this essay or story about a hunting expedition was considered good enough by the teachers that it was to be printed whether it appealed to me or not."[6] In the story, a Cree Indian named Pierre believes that his trapping partner, Dick Haywood, has stolen his wallet. To exact revenge, Pierre sets a snare for Haywood along the trail the two usually followed. Starting out "over the crust with the swinging snowshoe stride of the traveller of the barren grounds," Haywood leaves to check the traps in temperatures approaching forty-two degrees below zero.[7] Meanwhile, Pierre waits in the cabin, gloating "evilly" to himself about his clever scheme to catch Dick like a rabbit. Upon accidentally discovering that the real thief is a red squirrel, however, Pierre, coatless and gloveless, madly runs into the woods to release his partner. By the time Pierre reaches the trap, Haywood's body has been mauled by a band of hungry timber wolves and two ravens pick "at the shapeless something that had once been Dick Haywood" (97). Distraught, the Cree Indian steps backward into the bear trap that Dick had come out to check. He stoically accepts his fate as the judgment of Manitou, the Ottawa word for God,[8] and reaches for his rifle to "save My-in-gau, the wolf, the trouble" of killing him (97).

The second story, "A Matter of Colour," appeared in April 1916 and is narrated by a character with an insider's knowledge of the boxing circuit. As is the case with "Judgment of Manitou," "A Matter of Colour" recounts a setup gone bad. Trainer Bob Armstrong tells a novice boxer how he had matched an up-and-coming lightweight, Montana Dan Morgan, against Joe Gans, "a pusson of color" and the current champion. Shortly before the fight, however, Morgan breaks his "right mauler," his only true weapon, and the match is in jeopardy. Armstrong, who has bet heavily on his fighter and stands to lose another five hundred dollars because of a forfeit clause, concocts a scheme to salvage the fight. The ring at the Olympic is on a stage with an old drop curtain in back, so Armstrong hires a "Big Swede" to stand behind the curtain. When Morgan maneuvers the black fighter into position, the Swede is supposed to knock out Gans with a baseball bat (99). But at the moment of truth, the Swede inexplicably clubs the wrong man, sending Morgan down for the count. When Armstrong incredulously asks "Why in the name of the Prophet did you hit the white man instead of the black one?" the Swede innocently replies "Mr. Armstrong, you should no talk at me like that—I bane color blind" (100).

In perhaps the most fully realized of the three high school stories, "Sepi Jingan," Hemingway returned to a northern woods setting for an adventure tale. An unidentified boy hears a story told by an Indian, Billy Tabeshaw, about how he was saved from death by his loyal dog, Sepi Jingan. Paul Black Bird, a "bad Indian" who "was crazy because he couldn't get drunk," had killed Billy's cousin, a game warden (102). Although the local sheriff tried to catch him, "there never was a white man yet could catch an Indian in the Indian's own country" (102). As a result, Billy says he took it upon himself to track Paul through Canada and Michigan to avenge the murder. After losing the scent of the killer, Billy recalls how he was surprised by Paul, who blindsided him in the Upper Peninsula woods with a pikepole. Billy says that as Paul stood menacingly over him, prepared to kill his pursuer, Sepi Jingan snuck behind the renegade Indian. The dog "sprang like a shaggy thunderbolt" toward Paul, snapping his neck between his "wolf jaws" and killing the attacker instantly (103). At the conclusion of his story, Billy boasts of making neat work of the death by placing Paul's body on the Pere Marquette track, removing all traces of the manner of his death and causing people to conclude erroneously that Paul Black Bird had drunkenly fallen asleep on the tracks.

As he did with his Ring Lardner takeoffs in the *Trapeze,* the newspaper of Oak Park and River Forest High School, Hemingway probably used some of the writers he had read as a student as models for his three stories. As Michael Reynolds has noted, "Because imitation came easy for him, he practiced it throughout his seven-year apprenticeship."[9] Hemingway's parody of Sherwood Anderson's *Dark Laughter* in *The Torrents of Spring* is but one of the many examples of his mutability as a young writer; Hemingway also modeled some of his unpublished attempts at "popular" fiction during 1919–21 on such writers as E. W. Howe.[10] In a similar manner, all three of the high school stories seem to be the products of Hemingway's ability to imitate writers for a particular purpose. For example, Jeffrey Meyers indicates that "the double death in 'The Judgment of Manitou' suggests Kipling's 'At the End of Passage'; the surprise ending in the boxing story 'A Matter of Colour' suggests O. Henry; the savage vengeance in 'Sepi Jingan' suggests the adventure tales of Jack London."[11] The London influence seems particularly poignant in the "man and dog" story and is also evident in "Judgment of Manitou," if for no other reason than its image of a trapper traveling through the north woods in subzero temperatures. As Reynolds has thoroughly documented, Hemingway's early reading has its roots primarily in nineteenth-century British literature, but Hemingway also avidly read London's short stories and *The Call of the Wild,* though his parents apparently "considered London too coarse and violent for the home library."[12] Unable to find the types of hunting expeditions to which he was accustomed in writers such as Chaucer or Spenser, two of the staples in the Oak Park curriculum, Hemingway turned to one of the few American models available to him in the Oak Park library to create his first adventure stories.[13]

Since he so frequently used the moniker *Ring Lardner, Jr.* in his columns for the *Trapeze,* it seems little surprise that Hemingway also would find him a ready model for the creation of a boxing story like "A Matter of Colour." Although he denigrated Lardner's writing as "illiterate" by 1933, Hemingway had placed Lardner's work "as high as Jupiter on tiptoes" in 1918.[14] The parallels to Lardner are obvious in Hemingway's earliest boxing story, particularly through the use of colloquial language and the way in which Hemingway makes Armstrong a confidential storyteller.

There are echoes of Hemingway's narrator in any number of Lardner's sketches that appeared in *The Saturday Evening Post* and the 1916 collection *You Know Me, Al*. By opening his story with Bob Armstrong's "What, you never heard the story about Joe Gan's first fight?" Hemingway borrowed a style for which Lardner was well noted. In his preface to *How to Write Short Stories* in 1924, Lardner said, "Personally it has been my observation that the reading public prefers short dialogue to any other kind of writing and I always aim to open my tale with two or three lines of conversation. . . . I have often found that something one of these characters says . . . directs my plot into channels deeper than I had planned and changes, for the better, the entire sense of my story."[15] In his early imitations of Lardner's work, Hemingway engendered the same philosophy, especially in stories such as "The Mercenaries."

But even as a high school writer, Hemingway did more than merely imitate other writers to create the basis for his work. All three *Tabula* pieces reflect Hemingway's early decision to write about what he knew best. Writing based on personal experience or close observation, of course, defined the content of his later fiction. Whether characters appeared in the form of bullfighting afficionados, wartime ambulance drivers, or relentless outdoorsmen, Hemingway frequently drew fictional starting points from his own life. Although perhaps wholly imaginative, the high school stories encompass terrain and subject matter that would have been familiar to the young Hemingway. In the case of "A Matter of Colour," with prevalent use of insider lingo to re-create the atmosphere of a Chicago gym, Hemingway might have drawn on his experiences as a novice boxer. One Hemingway legend purports that in the winter of his junior year, shortly before the publication of his second story, he signed up for boxing lessons at a local gym. He eagerly attended the first Saturday lesson and promptly was knocked senseless, as were the other students in attendance. It was a confidence game based on the assumption that no students would be willing to come back the following week. But Hemingway returned, allegedly learning enough rudimentary skills to knock out a parade of reluctant friends in

Grace's music room.[16] Fenton substantiated the national interest in boxing during this era by writing that "every town in America had its gym and its stable of aspiring thugs" during the first two decades of the twentieth century.[17] While this might be hyperbole, the protracted search for the Great White Hope and Teddy Roosevelt's love for the sport probably helped to provide the basis for Hemingway's interest in boxing during his high school years, eventually leading to "A Matter of Colour."

The foundation of the other two stories clearly comes from Hemingway's experience in northern Michigan. Since "Judgment of Manitou" takes place in the Ungava region in nearby Ontario, northern Michigan probably served as the model for the setting of the story. Hemingway's attention to detail regarding cultural folklore in the story indicates that he made use of legends he had heard from Native American acquaintances. For example, Montgomery believes that "Hemingway's use of the Indian word 'Ojibway' (an alternate spelling which Hemingway used) instead of the 'white man's' word, 'Chippewa,' " for the local tribe in the story is "further evidence that his association with the Indians was personal and direct."[18] The use of words like *Kootzie-ootzie* (the "little bad god of the Crees") reinforces that connection.

Hemingway's relationship with the local tribe appears even more vividly in "Sepi Jingan." Since the allusion to the Pere Marquette tracks and the Lower Peninsula places the story near Walloon Lake, Hemingway examined familiar terrain to create his final high school story. In writing about someone he knew personally, Billy Tabeshaw (who also appears as a fictional character in "Ten Indians" and "The Doctor and the Doctor's Wife"), Hemingway perhaps recounted a tall tale Billy had once told him. Montgomery observed, "In this more sophisticated story, Hemingway had the same clarity of narrative and certainty of style that he always had when he knew the subject from first-hand experience and had not created it out of his imagination."[19] That "Sepi Jingan" is a story within a story further suggests Hemingway might have been "reporting" a local legend. The death of Paul Black Bird on the railroad tracks, for example, might have emerged from several stories Hemingway heard while a teenager in Michigan. The father of one of his friends, Tommy Mitchell, "was one of the drunken Indians who passed out on the railroad tracks and was run over by a train."[20] Another incident recalls a "very tall Indian who had given Ernest a canoe paddle made from ashwood" and who rented a cabin on a neighbor's farm.[21] Baker writes that "the manner of his death was memorable. One Fourth of July he went to Petoskey to celebrate by getting drunk. On the way home he fell asleep on the Pere Marquette railway tracks and was run over by the midnight train."[22] This information comes from an unpublished Nick Adams fragment with an uncertain composition date, perhaps Hemingway's recollection of his earlier high school story.

With these initial efforts to present stories in a distanced, journalistic style, young Ernest Hemingway was experimenting with a narrative method he periodically used in his later career. In both "Sepi Jingan" and "A Matter of Colour," a narrator simply recounts what those with an insider's knowledge have experienced. The "reporter" is not part of the action itself, and he does not comment on what he has heard. In this manner, the stories could then be told by people very much unlike Hemingway. At the same time, this style creates individual characterization without the need for intrusive comment or lengthy description. Later works like "After the Storm" and "The Mother of a Queen" use this same method through a narrator who confides in the reader. In a letter to Arnold Gingrich in the spring before the publication of *Winner Take Nothing*, Hemingway claimed that several of the stories in his new collection were taken directly from various sources. Hemingway told Gingrich that he wrote "some stories absolutely as they happen i.e. Wine of Wyoming—the letter one ["One Reader Writes"], and another ["After the Storm"] word for word as it happened to Bra, The Mother of a Queen, Gambler, Nun, Radio. . . . Others I invent completely—Killers, Hills Like White Elephants, The Undefeated, Fifty Grand, Sea Change, A Simple Enquiry. *Nobody* can tell which ones I make up completely."[23] In "After the Storm," Hemingway used a story originally told by Bra Saunders; bullfighter Sidney Franklin was the likely prototype for Roger, the acerbic narrator in "The Mother of a Queen."

This blend of reporting and fictionalizing especially seems apparent in the clarity of Billy Tabeshaw's character in "Sepi Jingan." Proficient in first-person narratives throughout his career, Hemingway consistently tried to find different voices for his dramatic monologues. Beginning with the young narrator in "My Old Man" and Jack Brennan in "Fifty Grand," and continuing through Pilar's vivid tales in *For Whom the Bell Tolls,* Hemingway invented a rich diversity of dramatic narrators. Beginning with his apprenticeship as a high school writer and his sketches written shortly after the war, Hemingway frequently experimented with this method. In his study of Hemingway's "Chicago manuscripts," Paul Smith noted the continual development of Hemingway's use of the dramatic monologue during his apprenticeship. In what Smith terms the Chicago style, the narrator typically "is an intermediary; he stands between his audience and the unfamiliar scene and characters he observes, but he has the credentials of a trusted listener. He is an inside witness."[24] The narrator shows worldliness and an insider's knowledge of the situation or character at hand by revealing the story in a style loosely based on that of Lardner or Kipling.

In the high school first-person narratives, Hemingway creates the characterization of an "inside witness" by close attention to the spoken word. His ability to convert oral language into dialogue appears to have emerged before he made a visit to another country. The high school stories indicate that his ability to hear local dialect helped him begin to understand how to develop a strong sense of individual personality for his characters. As an observer in Chicago gyms, for example, "His interest in boxing may well have prompted him to make a few Saturday morning visits to Forbes and Feretti's or Kid Howard's just to see how it was done. If he kept his eyes and ears open and listened to yarns by some of the old guard, there was always a chance of fresh material for short stories."[25] In these gyms, or perhaps through Lardner's newspaper columns, Hemingway might have picked up boxing lingo like "dockwalloper," "ten-second anesthetic," and "you couldn't punch a ripple in a bowl of soup," all phrases used by trainer Bob Armstrong in "A Matter of Colour." Such terminology captures the Chicago tough-guy insider Hemingway probably would have encountered during his boxing lessons. Dick Haywood's "Holy quill pigs!" in response to the bitter temperatures is but one of the idiomatic phrases in "Judgment of Manitou." The renderings through dialogue of the Cree Indian Pierre in "Judgment of Manitou," the Big Swede in "A Matter of Colour," and Billy Tabeshaw in "Sepi Jingan" all reveal varied explorations of capturing local color and perhaps suggest the early influence of Mark Twain's *Adventures of Huckleberry Finn*. In particular, by having his "Sepi Jingan" narrator emphasize that Billy "is not the redskin of the popular magazine," Hemingway showed he was not interested on falling back on worn clichés but rather in capturing language as he himself had heard it. The narrator of "Sepi Jingan" adds that "I have yet to hear him grunt or speak of the Great White Father at Washington" (101). Such a statement might emphasize that the young Ernest Hemingway's close contact with Native Americans in Michigan allowed him to transcend imitative stereotypes. Matthew Bruccoli stresses that the stories "reveal that the young Hemingway had an awareness of the technique of fiction—in particular, of the development of character through speech."[26] Hemingway's prevalent use of local dialect in all three of his high school stories anticipates his later attempts to capture Spanish inflection in works like *For Whom the Bell Tolls*, "A Clean, Well-Lighted Place," and *The Old Man and the Sea*.

The subject matter of the high school stories, especially regarding brutal justice, reveals much about Hemingway's fascination with violence long before any traumatic experiences in Italy. All three of the high school stories contain various forms of violent trauma, beginning with the murder-suicide in "Judgment of Manitou," continuing through the seemingly comical clubbing of Montana Dan Morgan in "A Matter of Colour," and concluding with Billy's apparent self-defense murder of Paul Black Bird in "Sepi Jingan." More important, the effect of violence on an individual observer, so much a part of Nick Adams stories like "The

Battler," "The Killers," and "Big Two-Hearted River," appears in all three of the *Tabula* stories, confirming "that Hemingway, before any traumatic experience in his life, had already begun to work toward the grammar of violence and death that marked his later work."[27] As Phillip Young noted, Hemingway protagonists often achieve stoic initiation upon observing the residue of violence; this particular aspect of the Hemingway code first emerges in "Sepi Jingan." The unnamed narrator's reaction to Billy Tabeshaw's braggadocio about Paul Black Bird's death is strangely shrouded at the end of the story. As Gerry Brenner has noted, when Billy remarks "Funny, ain't it?" at the conclusion of his tale, the narrator does not respond or bid Billy farewell as he leaves. Brenner believes that this nonresponsiveness creates the same sense of ambivalence and ambiguity that shrouds Nick Adams's numbed reaction to Ad Francis at the end of "The Battler."[28] Brenner poses several possibilities to account for the narrator's silence: his reverent awe, fear of the burden of responsibility involved with knowing the truth of Paul's death, disgust with the brutality on both sides, or possibly a recognition of Billy's self-aggrandizement. On the other hand, Bruccoli argues that "it is not difficult to see Billy Tabeshaw as a Hemingway code hero."[29] What ultimately is important is that the narrator's reaction toward Billy is unknown, establishing an early use of the ambiguity that marks Hemingway's best work. A similar argument might be made for the reaction of the listener-reporter toward Bob Armstrong in "A Matter of Colour" upon the discovery that the trainer is capable of promoting a crooked fight for monetary gain.

At the same time, a sense of clear justice also accompanies the violence in the three stories. The betrayal of friendship that results in the murder of his partner can create only one ending for Pierre in "Judgment of Manitou." In a similar manner, Paul Black Bird, murderer of a game warden who merely tried to stop him from fishing illegally, ironically meets the justifiable end with which he threatens Billy and Sepi. Although Paul says "I will kill you both and then slide you onto the rails" (102), he is the one on the Pere Marquette tracks at the end of the story. The endings of both of these early stories represent an eye-for-an-eye karma that is perhaps more simplistic in its morality than some of Hemingway's later works, although violation of an unspoken code often creates some form of retribution. Jake Barnes's loss of friendship with Montoya because of his role in the Brett Ashley–Pedro Romero romance is but one example of reparation.

As Gregory Green has shown, the equities of "A Matter of Colour" are potentially more convoluted but nonetheless evident in a historical context.[30] Green argues that Hemingway's story was, in part, a response to racist attitudes behind the demand for a Great White Hope to wrest the heavyweight championship away from Chicagoan Jack Johnson, the first African-American champion. Green's first reference point is a boxing anecdote about Stanley Ketchel, whom Hemingway later fictionalized in "Light of the World." While on the "theater circuit" at the beginning of his career, Ketchel reputedly had opponents clubbed with a lead pipe when the situation warranted. Green's use of this story leads to speculation regarding the famous 1909 Johnson–Ketchel title bout that saw white America urging Ketchel to recapture the belt. Green sees that the racism involved with the fight seemingly "divided Hemingway between a desire to impose justice on an unjust world and an equally strong desire to witness man triumph when all the odds are all on the other side."[31] The ending of "A Matter of Colour" might then be seen as a moral reversal. The deserving Joe Gans (who, Hemingway carefully points out, eventually becomes the lightweight champion of the world) emerges as the winner of the fight because of color blindness not evident in society as a whole. While perhaps overcrediting Hemingway's subtlety as a high school writer, Green believes he restored "blind justice to a world that, sadly enough, for a sixteen year old boy from Chicago, did not share the big Swede's affliction. Hemingway makes the club swing the other way and the black fighter, given his opportunity, goes on to become champion of the world."[32] The professional and deserving fighter, therefore, wins despite the cheap slapstick tricks of Morgan and Armstrong. Fenton's "No Money for the Kingbird" further illustrates Hemingway's feelings about "professionalism" and abhorrence for the "amateur." Although Fenton primarily focuses on later stories like "Fifty Grand" and Hemingway's *Esquire* article on the Max Baer–Joe Louis fight, "A Matter of Colour" can be seen as an early expression of Hemingway's belief in the need for professionalism to triumph over trickery. In a world composed of Hemingway's justice, those who rely on deceit, such as Montana Dan Morgan, the trapper Pierre, and Paul Black Bird, lose to the apparently more deserving.

Attributing the qualities of Hemingway's later works to the stories he wrote as a high school student would be overreading these early efforts. For example, with a few rare exceptions, the O. Henry surprise twists in all three stories do not indicate the type of ending Hemingway generally used in his more mature writing. This convention, also a part of the Chicago style between 1919 and 1921, gradually gave way to a more understated eloquence in his later works. The Kipling-style, straightforward narratives of the three stories do not anticipate the more experimental fiction of the 1920s, in which Hemingway employed a kind of "nonnarrative" in works like "Now I Lay Me" and "In Another Country." Hemingway's apprenticeship reveals remarkable stylistic changes in his writing leading up to the famous Paris "true sentences" in 1922. Nonetheless, by providing an early perspective of a writer who achieved international fame, the value of these stories seems undeniable. While many of the techniques and themes attributed to events in Hemingway's later life contributed to his development as a writer, it is clear that important aspects of his subjects and style were established long before he felt shrapnel in Italy, was spurned in love, or spoke with some of the literary masters of his day.

NOTES

1. Carlos Baker, ed., *Ernest Hemingway: Selected Letters 1917–1961* (New York: Charles Scribner's Sons, 1981), 787.

2. Matthew J. Bruccoli, ed., *Ernest Hemingway's Apprenticeship: Oak Park, 1916–1917* (New York: Microcard Editions, 1971), xiv.

3. Carlos Baker, *Ernest Hemingway: A Life Story* (New York: Scribners, 1969), 27.

4. As Michael Reynolds notes in his introduction to *Critical Essays on Ernest Hemingway's* In Our Time (Boston: G. K. Hall & Co., 1983), some of Hemingway's postwar, pre-Paris sketches run into problems because of a lack of dialogue. At the urging of Bill Smith, and under the influence of E. W. Howe's "The Anthology of Another Town" in the *Saturday Evening Post,* Hemingway began to let his characters again speak for themselves.

5. Constance Cappel Montgomery, *Hemingway in Michigan* (New York: Fleet Publishing Corporation, 1966), 43.

6. Montgomery, *Hemingway in Michigan,* 43.

7. Bruccoli, *Ernest Hemingway's Apprenticeship,* 96. All subsequent references to the *Tabula* stories will be to this edition.

8. Hemingway might have been familiar with this word because one of the Lake Michigan steamers on which the Hemingways traveled was the *Manitou.*

9. Michael S. Reynolds, *The Young Hemingway* (New York: Basil Blackwell, 1986), 49.

10. Michael S. Reynolds, *Critical Essays on Ernest Hemingway's* In Our Time, 4.

11. Jeffrey Meyers, *Hemingway: A Biography* (New York: Harper & Row, 1985), 19–20.

12. James Mellow, *Hemingway: A Life without Consequences* (New York: Houghton Mifflin Company, 1992), 23.

13. In creating either "Sepi Jingan" or "Judgment of Manitou," Hemingway also might have been expressing his admiration for Rudyard Kipling's "insider's knowledge of things and his fascination with men of moral fortitude on the verge of collapse." Kenneth Lynn, *Hemingway* (New York: Simon and Schuster, 1987), 61.

14. Baker, *Ernest Hemingway: A Life Story,* 51.

15. Maxwell Geismar, ed., *The Ring Lardner Reader* (New York: Charles Scribner's Sons, 1963), 637.

16. This Hemingway anecdote appears in at least two different sources: Peter Griffin, *Along with Youth: Hemingway, the Early Years* (Oxford: Oxford University Press, 1985), 23–24, and Charles Fenton, "No Money for the Kingbird: Hemingway's Prizefight Stories," *American Quarterly* 4 (Winter 1952): 339–50.

17. Fenton, "No Money for the Kingbird," 339.

18. Montgomery, *Hemingway in Michigan,* 46–47.

19. Montgomery, *Hemingway in Michigan,* 50.

20. Montgomery, *Hemingway in Michigan,* 93.

21. Baker, *Hemingway: A Life Story,* 13.

22. In an endnote, Baker adds, however, that "the tall Indian killed by the train may have been an invention of EH's" (568).

23. Baker, ed., *Ernest Hemingway: Selected Letters,* 393.

24. Paul Smith, "Hemingway's Apprentice Fiction: 1919–1921," *American Literature,* 58 (December 1986): 574–88.

25. Baker, *Ernest Hemingway: A Life Story,* 22–23.

26. Bruccoli, *Ernest Hemingway's Apprenticeship,* xiv.

27. Mellow, *Hemingway,* 26.

28. Gerry Brenner, "From 'Sepi Jingan' to 'The Mother of a Queen': Hemingway's Three Epistemologic Formulas for Short Fiction," in *New Critical Approaches to the Short Stories of Ernest Hemingway,* ed. Jackson J. Benson (Durham: Duke University Press, 1990), 156–71.

29. Bruccoli, *Ernest Hemingway's Apprenticeship,* xiv.

30. Gregory Green, " 'A Matter of Color': Hemingway's Criticism of Race Prejudice,' " *Hemingway Review* 1 (Fall 1981): 27–32.

31. Green, " 'A Matter of Color,' " 31.

32. Green, " 'A Matter of Color,' " 30.

CARLOS AZEVEDO

Oak Park as the Thing Left Out: Surface and Depth in "Soldier's Home"

IT MAY BE SAFELY STATED that, when confronted with the variety of interpretations they continue to evoke, Ernest Hemingway's stories are a tantalizing, never-surrendering enigma that, like Francis Macomber (an exceptional case of an Oak Park name sliding into Hemingway's fiction),[1] have always generated "a great tolerance which seemed the nicest thing about him if it were not the most sinister."[2] In Macomber's story, the object of his tolerance is his wife, "cheerful and quite lovely" (8), "enamelled in that American female cruelty" (9). In analyzing Hemingway's fiction, the critical interest it has generated must be regarded as a capital fact, encompassing debates and discoveries. The map to be made by critics and scholars will in itself indicate a certain degree of uneasiness Hemingway felt about the parochial context of Oak Park, where sinister instability, cruelty, and damage waited in ambush for him.

The center of family gravity in the evolution of the young Hemingway was located roughly in the period 1901–20: a month before his second birthday, a photograph of Ernest was taken in a gown and bonnet, suggestively captioned "summer girl"; in the summer of 1920, he was exposed to the "American female cruelty" of his mother, Grace Hall Hemingway, who drove him out of the family house in Michigan, punishing him for transgressions against the sacred principles of Oak Park. Thus, the roots

of Hemingway's confusion, anxiety, and irreverence, of his sub-
version of established modes, of his literary experiments and the
correlative theory of omission, lie in a family situation delineated
at a very early age. In Oak Park, in a household ruled by a domineering and obsessive mother, Hemingway experienced a suffocating sense of danger. As he put it bitterly in the "Ezra Pound
and His Bel Esprit" section of *A Moveable Feast,*

> If a man liked his friends' painting or writing, I thought it was
> probably like those people who like their families, and it was not
> polite to criticize them. Sometimes you can go quite a long time
> before you criticize families, your own or those by marriage, but
> it is easier with bad painters because they do not do terrible
> things and make intimate harm as families can do. With bad
> painters all you need to do is not look at them. But even when
> you have learned not to look at families nor listen to them and
> have learned not to answer letters, families have many ways of be-
> ing dangerous.[3]

The bitterness of growing up in a Homeric battlefield was
very real and became one of the foundations of Hemingway's
thought. Born into a respected and respectful Oak Park family
of high Victorian temper, young Ernest began to think of the
village world as a neighborhood of traditionalism that enclosed
him on all sides, religious, political, and cultural. On the surface
it was a stable world beyond which life did not seem to exist at
all. It was a repository of charming memories stimulated by old
Oak Parkers who had fought in the Civil War, when dreams of
valor and glory were still possible, and in the literature favored
in the Hemingway house. Church and family were the polar sym-
bols around which life in Oak Park could be said to exist. The
Hemingway household was female territory presided over by
Grace Hall Hemingway, a nemesis from whom Ernest (and his
tense, henpecked father) fled by going out into the masculine
territory of the rural outdoors, where a sense of freedom could
be exercised.

Because he was so completely bound up in these two contra-
dictory worlds, Ernest's extraordinary intensity turned upon his

native region, with the interlocked anguish and joy that are the expression of divided will. The biographies of Ernest Hemingway by Jeffrey Meyers, Michael S. Reynolds, and Kenneth Lynn, focusing on the relationship between the author's life and his writing, offer extraordinary revelations about Hemingway's sexual psychology and explain how Hemingway developed such a detached, hostile attitude toward women.[4] More specifically, in the case of Lynn's book, Hemingway as a young Oak Parker is portrayed as a good deal less of a macho cultist of sporting values and stoic poise than might be expected from a long series of specialized studies, conferences, academic dissertations, and mass-market paraphernalia. The effect is not to downplay the importance of war as a theme in Hemingway's work or to dismiss the war trauma theory, although it is often simplistically stated and analyzed. It is, however, imperative that a prewar trauma, a prewar revulsion, a prewar bias in the environmental pressures of Oak Park be carefully dealt with. Before Fossalta di Piave, Hemingway was, in his innermost self, a man whose imagination remained centrally possessed by the image of his mother.

Among other pieces of biographical evidence, Lynn argues that Hemingway was affected by gender anxiety as a consequence of his mother's dressing him as a girl and passing him off as the same-sex twin of his older sister, Marcelline. It is a fact that turn-of-the-century small boys often wore dresses, but it is also true that Grace Hall Hemingway dressed and coiffed her son as a girl for a significantly longer period than was usual. These two-and-a-half years of Hemingway's life deserve attention, and specific importance must be attached to the memoir written by Marcelline the year after Ernest committed suicide. She explained that her mother wanted the two children to look alike, to feel alike, to have everything alike. As Lynn observes, Marcelline and Ernest "slept in the same bedroom in twin white cribs; they had dolls that were just alike; they played with small china tea sets that had the same pattern. Later, the children were encouraged to fish together and visit friends together, and after Grace deliberately held Marcelline back, they entered grade school together."[5]

These maternal enthusiasms, in addition to challenging existing gender boundaries, pulled Hemingway toward a confused sexual identity his mother wanted to control. Grace Hall Hemingway sometimes had Marcelline's and Ernest's hair cut the same way, and this memory pushed him toward a fixation with hair associated with fantasies of sexual transference. In "Soldier's Home," most good-looking girls Harold Krebs liked to look at "had their hair cut short" (112). In *The Sun Also Rises,* Hemingway explores the fluctuations of gender identity, namely when Brett Ashley disagrees with Pedro Romero about her short hair and mannish hat. In *A Farewell to Arms,* Catherine Barkley suggests that she and Frederic get identical haircuts:

> "Darling, why don't you let your hair grow?"
> "How grow?"
> "Just grow a little longer."
> "It's long enough now."
> "No, let it grow a little longer and I could cut mine and we'd be just alike only one of us blonde and one of us dark."
> "I wouldn't let you cut yours."
> "It would be fun. I'm tired of it. It's an awful nuisance in the bed at night."
> "I like it."
> "Wouldn't you like it short?"
> "I might. I like it the way it is."
> "It might be nice short. Then we'd both be alike. Oh, darling, I want you so much I want to be you too."[6]

Similarly, Robert Jordan, in *For Whom the Bell Tolls,* proposes that he and Maria

> "go together to the coiffeur's and they could cut it neatly on the sides and in the back as they cut mine and that way it would look better in the town while it is growing out."
> "I would look like thee," she said and held him close to her. "And then I never would want to change it."[7]

This passage is merely a confirmation of Robert Jordan's and Maria's feelings some pages earlier:

"Afterwards we will be as one animal of the forest and be so close that neither one can tell that one of us is one and not the other. Can you not feel my heart be your heart?"

"Yes. There is no difference."

"Now, feel. I am thee and thou art me and all of one is the other." (262)

The fetishism involving hair length and Robert's suggestion that he and Maria be rendered indistinguishable are evidence of a transformational chain that recurs in Hemingway's fictions, even in those dating back to the twenties. It becomes clear that the effects of twinship produced by outward appearance imply an effective switching in sex and gender roles that constitutes the essence of Hemingway's erotic ideal.

In *Islands in the Stream,* "Thomas Hudson was asleep" and "he dreamed that his son Tom was not dead and that the other boys were all right and that the war was over. He dreamed that Tom's mother was sleeping with him and she was sleeping on top of him as she liked to do sometimes."[8] Once again, the woman takes the lead in erotic games:

"Should I be you or you be me?"

"You have first choice."

"I'll be you."

"I can't be you. But I can try."

"It's fun. You try it. Don't try to save yourself at all. Try to lose everything and take everything too." (344)

In *The Garden of Eden,* the American novelist David Bourne and his wife, Catherine, dress alike and sport identical short haircuts. She assumes the name "Peter" and calls her husband "Catherine." He calls her "brother"; they are taken by observers to be brother and sister. In "Soldier's Home," a love relationship is established between Harold Krebs and his tomboy sister, Helen, who says she "can pitch better than lots of the boys. I tell them all you taught me. The other girls aren't much good" (114). It is also significant that "Helen" was Hemingway's fictional name in the story "On Writing" for his own wife, Hadley Richardson, a situation that did not repeat itself in Hemingway's writing. But, as Bernard Oldsey points out, in one of the manuscripts of the story Hemingway wrote *Hadley* instead of *Helen*.[9]

Released from the decorum of Oak Park, Hemingway allowed himself to depict gender confusion in his fiction and to represent erotic inclinations his Oak Park education had repressed. As he once wrote to F. Scott Fitzgerald, "Forget your personal tragedy. We are all bitched from the start and you especially have to be hurt like hell before you can write seriously. But when you get the damned hurt use it—don't cheat with it. Be as faithful to it as a scientist—but don't think anything is of any importance because it happens to you or anyone belonging to you."[10] Hemingway never forgot the "personal tragedy" his upbringing initially suppressed, and he felt it was of the utmost importance. He tried hard to know how to use it.

From childhood onward, Hemingway instinctively began to omit his deeper feelings and the vagaries of his family life and to let only the tip of selected moveable surfaces show. He did so as a way of conduct and as a strategy for his own writing. Oak Park, which for Hemingway became more and more synonymous with Grace Hall Hemingway's ambitions, piety, possessiveness, and emotional demands, is the first place to look for an explanation of the oddities of the author's imagination and his theory of fiction. It is no matter of chance that in "Monologue to the Maestro: A High Seas Letter," when a young apprentice writer asked Hemingway "What is the best early training for a writer?" he answered "An unhappy childhood."[11]

As a journalist and as a writer in the Parisian milieu, he would later learn to prune that theory and to elaborate upon it in *Death in the Afternoon*: "If a writer of prose knows enough about what he is writing about he may omit things that he knows and the reader, if the writer is writing truly enough, will have a feeling of those things as strongly as though the writer had stated them. The dignity of movement of an iceberg is due to only one-eighth of it being above water."[12] Hemingway never wrote a single story about Oak Park, and none of his characters was brought up there, but biographically informed criticism points to something hidden. The absence of Oak Park actually masks an oppressive sense of its presence in his psychic world. Hemingway seems to have been trying to hide not merely the actual role that his mother had played in his life but the fact that she had a role at all. Such a denial only suggests that her role must have been very large indeed. On the other hand, in Hemingway's theory of omission, extratextual entities are cast in the roles of witness, critic, and judge. They must not merely witness but contribute to a debate or supply the meaning of a text themselves. In the case of Hemingway's short stories, it becomes evident that success depends as much on the critic's participation as it does on the author's words. The ability to hear deeper echoes between the lines depends on the critic's perception and on an ability to recognize implicit patterns of indeterminacy that allow for an interpretation of the text. Hemingway maneuvered his audience into cooperating with him in his performance. Among his short stories written in the early twenties, "Soldier's Home" constitutes one of the best examples of emotional understatement, of a deliberate strategy of leaving out relevant information, of providing blanks in the textual surface, requiring a creative interaction to grasp the depth of a complex web of relationships.

As Reynolds points out, Hemingway's "story of the returning veteran, 'Soldier's Home,' uses some of his own experience [in Oak Park] but he moved the locale to Oklahoma."[13] Harold Krebs, the boy "who had been a good soldier" (113) and "had done the one thing, the only thing for a man to do, easily and naturally" (111), is able to retain his integrity during the war. In contrast, he returns to a world that is corrupt, artificial, and hypocritical and in which he no longer feels at home. The irony of the title is a counterpoint to what Krebs felt, caught in the limbo between childhood and adulthood, stripped of any romanticism he may have had, nauseated by his mother's platitudes:

> "God has some work for every one to do," his mother said.
> "There can be no idle hands in His Kingdom."
> "I'm not in His Kingdom," Krebs said.
> "We are all of us in His Kingdom."
> Krebs felt embarrassed and resentful as always. (115)

In a famous passage in *A Farewell to Arms* that is usually taken as a fundamental expression of Hemingway's literary credo and of what lies behind his early style, Frederic Henry expresses his own nausea:

> I was always embarrassed by the words sacred, glorious, and sacrifice and the expression in vain. . . . I had seen nothing sacred, and the things that were glorious had no glory and the sacrifices were like the stockyards at Chicago if nothing was done with the meat except to bury it. There were many words that you could not stand to hear and finally only the names of places had dignity. . . . Abstract words such as glory, honor, courage, or hallow were obscene beside the concrete names of villages, the numbers of roads, the names of rivers, the numbers of regiments and the dates.[14]

If Krebs and Frederic Henry have always been embarrassed by the obscenity of abstractions, such may be the case because this strategy of abstractions is part of a rhetoric of intimidation and oppressiveness in Hemingway's early life. As in the case of his creator, Krebs's mind was ruled by the sense of what his mother had done and could do to him. Both mothers would very likely want their sons to remain dependent upon their demands and control. When Krebs's mother talks about temptations in wartime and Krebs looks down "at the bacon fat hardening on his plate" (115), he is once more trying to avoid embarrassment and to deflate a sense of conflict and tension that threatens his individual identity. "Soldier's Home" is a tale of individual affirmation and the loss of happiness and freedom in a female-ruled household. In Hemingway's stories about parents, as Richard Hovey observes, "The mothers regularly appear as domineering over their families; as destroyers, actual or potential, of their children; as champions of respectability and defenders of cruel sentimentalities and false values. Just as regularly, the fathers are depicted as weak; as men on whom sons dare not wholly rely."[15] Krebs's mother knows "how weak men are" (115), and Krebs's father is never present.

Hemingway's homecoming from the war, according to his sister Marcelline, "must have been something like being put in a box with the cover nailed down to come home to conventional, suburban Oak Park living."[16] In "Soldier's Home," Harold Krebs experiences a similar sense of uneasiness and alienation not because of a war trauma but, in all likelihood, as a consequence of a family trauma generated by his mother in the past. After all, unlike Krebs, his native region and what it stood for had not changed. Apparently, Krebs is not very successful in making his "Mummy" understand that he is no longer her little boy. He regrets his saying that he does not love her and hurriedly makes a promise: "I'll try and be a good boy for you" (116). This statement does not necessarily mean capitulation. Rather, it is an attempt to recognize his mother as a separate person with an autonomous existence and independent consciousness, something more than a figure in his own carpet. Krebs declares his independence when he symbolically chooses the world of his sister over the suffocating world of his mother. He decides to watch Helen play baseball rather than visit his father: "He would not go down to his father's office. He would miss that one. He wanted his life to go smoothly. It had just gotten going that way. Well, that was all over now, anyway. He would go over to the schoolyard and watch Helen play indoor baseball" (116). Indoor rather than outdoor baseball seems to suggest that Helen's realm stands for shelter and protection. It is an alternative world, a refuge from the confusion his mother implants in his mind. This interference deprives the son of a solid sexual identity, a fact that manifests itself in the incestuous overtones of the relationship between Harold and Helen. He experiences his attachment to another woman as enacting some sort of killing revenge on his mother. Helen asks Harold if he is her beau and he replies: "Sure. You're my girl now" (114).

In this accurate, though necessarily figural, dramatization of Hemingway's inner reality, the parallel with the author's own deep attachment to his younger sister, Ursula, seems evident. As a consequence of his being forced into dressing exactly like Marcelline, Hemingway despised her. The quasi-romantic feelings he possessed for Ursula (almost certainly the model for Harold's sister) represent an effort to reject a pattern his mother tried to impose and are themselves evidence of Hemingway's gender trouble. In "Soldier's Home" Helen herself helps to maintain this type of incestuous identity. She asks Harold to watch her play softball, telling him, "If you loved me, you'd want to come over and watch me play indoor" (115). Significantly, the girls described in the story form "a pattern" (112). They all dress exactly alike, much as Harold and his fraternity brothers wear "exactly the same height and style collar" (111). The girls "lived in such a complicated world of already defined alliances and shifting feuds that Krebs did not feel the energy or the courage to break into it" (112). This uniformity constitutes one of the reasons for Harold's strong attachment to Helen: she represents a world far more sensible and genuine than the sterile world of the town. If the community does not offer him a sense of place, Helen brings back a center and, through her affection, seems to validate her brother's maleness. But if the girls are the picture of conformity, the picture that shows Harold in Europe wearing an ill-fitting uniform symbolically captures his inability to validate his war experience and to live up to the adult ranks of male dominance.

After returning from the war, Krebs discovers that to be heard, he has to invent lies that deprived the experiences he had had of any meaning and caused severe damage: "Krebs acquired the nausea in regard to experience that is the result of untruth or exaggeration" (112). Looking at the future he tries to delineate for himself, Krebs declares his intentions: "He did not want to get into the intrigue and the politics. He did not want to have to do any courting. He did not want to tell any more lies. It wasn't worth it" (113). He obviously tells lies, even in his affectionate relationship with Helen:

"Am I really your girl?"
"Sure."
"Do you love me?"
"Uh, huh."
"Will you love me always?"
"Sure." (114)

He does not want any consequences, but his life will obviously have them. To circumvent them, he has to find a pattern to cope with a world in which his mother waits in ambush for him. The fear lurking behind "Soldier's Home" concerns an urgency about maintaining control. Harold Krebs may escape into a poolroom, a book, or a schoolyard, but these evasions are partial and transitory. Freedom, in the ecstatic sense that he experiences, could hardly be had in his hometown or, for that matter, in any other known human society. Hemingway's and Krebs's problems are the disparity between their best impulses and the behavior that communities and mothers attempted to impose upon them. The result is that, in "Soldier's Home," Krebs makes a move for freedom from the community's mold and from the underlying motherly code. The direction in which he is propelled implies his reading of the war, the discovery of a meaning for his past, and the need for "more maps" (113) to visualize a future with consequences.

Harold Krebs escapes from a world of danger, embarrassment, and nausea and finds refuge among the ritual symmetry of sport, his ultimate best hope for an unmapped future. Unlike some short stories, such as "The Battler," "Fifty Grand," or "My Old Man" or the fixed horse race in *A Farewell to Arms,* sport in Krebs's imagination is uncorrupted and uncorruptible, a haven located somewhere between the present and the future. The story is filled with suggestiveness and must be read in the light of a severe psychological disturbance that has always embarrassed Hemingway. "Soldier's Home" provides an example of a story that cannot be deciphered without referring to extratextual elements. Hemingway wrote it under the tension caused by the wound inflicted by Oak Park. Hemingway privileged the tension and the attempt to overcome it, not the "thing" that caused the tension. He left the thing out: Oak Park is not above water.

The end of this closely autobiographical story provides an exit for Harold Krebs that has a meaning—sport. Hemingway himself, beyond the ambiguity of his fiction, escaped the priggish pattern of his boyhood by embracing a career as a writer. But wherever he went, and under whatever kind of mask, responsible only to himself and his art, the psychic map of Oak Park remained uppermost in Hemingway's mind. It is too vast a map to be deciphered, but in the foreseeable future, more and more attention will be given to Oak Park and its place in Hemingway territory.

NOTES

1. See Michael S. Reynolds, "Macomber: An Old Oak Park Name," *Hemingway Review* 3 (Fall 1983): 28–29. See also Michael S. Reynolds, *The Young Hemingway* (Oxford: Blackwell, 1986), 52.

2. Ernest Hemingway, "The Short Happy Life of Francis Macomber," in *The Complete Short Stories of Ernest Hemingway: The Finca Vigia Edition* (New York: Scribners, 1987), 18. All subsequent references to Hemingway's short stories are to this edition and will be cited in the text.

3. Ernest Hemingway, *A Moveable Feast* (New York: Scribners, 1964), 107–8.

4. Jeffrey Meyers, *Hemingway: A Biography* (New York: Harper & Row, 1985); Reynolds, *The Young Hemingway;* Kenneth S. Lynn, *Hemingway* (New York: Simon and Schuster, 1987).

5. Lynn, *Hemingway*, 41–42.

6. Ernest Hemingway, *A Farewell to Arms* (New York: Scribners, 1929), 299.

7. Ernest Hemingway, *For Whom the Bell Tolls* (New York: Scribners, 1940), 345.

8. Ernest Hemingway, *Islands in the Stream* (New York: Scribners, 1970), 343.

9. Bernard Oldsey, "Hemingway's Beginnings and Endings," *College Literature* 7, No. 3 (1980): 219.

10. Carlos Baker, ed., *Ernest Hemingway: Selected Letters, 1917–1961* (New York: Scribners, 1981), 408.

11. William White, ed., *By-Line: Ernest Hemingway* (New York: Scribners, 1967), 219.

12. Ernest Hemingway, *Death in the Afternoon* (New York: Scribners, 1932), 192.

13. Reynolds, *The Young Hemingway*, 52.

14. Hemingway, *A Farewell to Arms*, 184–85.

15. Richard B. Hovey, *Hemingway: The Inward Terrain* (Seattle: University of Washington Press, 1968), 43.

16. Marcelline Hemingway Sanford, *At the Hemingways: A Family Portrait* (Boston: Little, Brown, 1962), 184.

Romantic Betrayal
in "Ten Indians"

THOUGH ERNEST HEMINGWAY was born and raised in Oak Park, Illinois, his artistic and spiritual home place was Walloon Lake, Michigan, where his family would vacation every summer. Here he learned to fish, hunt, swim, and paddle a canoe, and he gained an appreciation of nature and a knowledge of wildlife. He would also be influenced by the Ottawa and Ojibwa Indians living nearby. According to Carlos Baker, "Although Ernest worshipped no heroes among the Indians who lived in the woods near Bacon's farm, he was constantly aware of their presence, like ata-vistic shadows moving along the edges of his consciousness, com-ing and going without a sound."[1] Indeed, the Indians and their country had a profound effect on Hemingway's imagination. From his first attempts at fiction and in his later Nick Adams sto-ries, he would draw upon his experiences at Walloon Lake, using Indian characters and wilderness settings. Yet he would not ide-alize the locale or the people here; the woods are not a remote Eden, untainted by the city's corruption, and the Indians are not portrayed as noble savages. Instead, Hemingway shows the wil-derness being destroyed and, with the loss of the trees, the end of the Indian way of life.

This fallen world is the setting of "Ten Indians," a story that centers on the adolescent Nick Adams's first disappointment in love as he learns that his Indian girlfriend, Prudence Mitchell, has been unfaithful.[2] The story includes two parts: the first is an account of Nick and the Garner family's ride home from a Fourth of July celebration in Petoskey; the second takes place in the Adamses' cabin, where Nick's father is waiting up for him. As Nick eats leftover chicken and huckleberry pie, Dr. Adams tells him that he saw Prudence Mitchell "threshing around" in the bushes with Frank Washburn (256). A tearful Nick goes to bed and lies face down on the pillow, thinking, "If I feel this way my heart must be broken" (257). The next morning, "There was a big wind blowing and the waves were running high up on the beach and he was awake a long time before he remembered that his heart was broken" (257). Nick, however, is not only saddened by the loss of his first love; he is also becoming aware of the loss of the forest and the old ways. He is beginning to see the harsh reality of the lives of the woods Indians, whose livelihood was being destroyed as the logging industry declined. As his infatuation with Prudence is ended, so too is his romantic idealization of the Indians and the wilderness way of life.

Many of the characters in "Ten Indians" are modeled after people Hemingway knew at Walloon Lake. The Garners are based on the Bacons, a family who lived on a farm near the Hemingways' lake house. In the first manuscripts of the story, Hemingway used the Bacons' real name.[3] Furthermore, the Bacons, like the Garners, had a son named Carl who was a friend of Ernest's. Billy Tabeshaw, who is mentioned in "Ten Indians," lived in the Indian camp near the Hemingway cottage. Prudence Mitchell is modeled after Prudence Boulton, the daughter of Richard Boulton, a half-breed sawyer fictionalized in "The Doctor and the Doctor's Wife." Prudence was two years younger than Ernest and worked for a time in the Hemingways' kitchen. Mary Hemingway recalled that when she first met Ernest, he told her that she had legs just like Prudy Boulton's, the "first female he had ever pleasured." However, Ernest's sister Sunny claimed that she never believed any of the stories about Ernest and Prudence: "I never saw any evidence of Ernie's liking her or even wanting her along on our exploring trips or squirrel-hunting jaunts." Carlos Baker concurred, believing that Ernest's affair with Prudence was more likely "the product of wishful thinking than fact." Although in the story "Fathers and Sons" Nick Adams remembers her as the one "who did first what no one has ever done better," the truth of this matter has never been ascertained.[4]

It cannot be proven that Hemingway knew that Prudence committed suicide in 1918, for he never wrote of her death and there is no record of his mentioning it to anyone. Hemingway visited Michigan in late April and early May 1918, and he returned three times between June and late August of 1919. Moreover, he lived in Petoskey from late October to December 1919. Paul Smith speculates, "If neither his close friend, Dutch Pailthorpe, nor the newspaper accounts revealed her death, it was perhaps an unusual stroke of luck."[5] Still, something upset Hemingway on May 16, 1926, when he was revising the story. In an interview with George Plimpton, Hemingway recounted the events of that productive day when the San Isidro bullfights were snowed out: "First I wrote 'The Killers,' which I'd tried to write before and failed. Then after lunch I got in bed to keep warm and wrote 'Today is Friday.' I had so much juice I thought maybe I was going crazy and I had about six other stories to write. So I got dressed and walked to Fornos, the old bullfighter's cafe, and drank coffee and then came back and wrote 'Ten Indians.' This made me very sad and I drank some brandy and went to sleep."[6] Granted, his marital problems undoubtedly added to his feeling of despair at this time, but he could also have been remembering the tragic death of Prudence. Although the extent of Hemingway's knowledge of Prudence's death is unknown, it is clear that she left a lasting impression on his life and works. She is featured in both "Ten Indians" and "Fathers and Sons," although in the latter work her name is Trudy Gilby. Trudy Gilby would again appear as an important character in "The Last Good Country," which Hemingway worked on intermittently between April 1952 and July 1958.

Prudence is just one of the many Indians who affected Hemingway. His curiosity about the Indians was an interest shared by his father. Clarence Hemingway had spent time at a Dakota Sioux reservation as a young man and passed down Indian lore to his son.[7] Clarence had a collection of Indian artifacts and could even make fire with the old flints he had found. Marcelline Hemingway Sanford reported that her father also kept in his office beaded moccasins, articles of decorated deerskin, and Indian baskets, many of which came from the Dakotas, where Mary Hemingway's (Uncle Will's wife's) twin sisters taught in an Indian mission school. Marcelline wrote that when her father was younger, he pretended that he and his brothers were members of a mythical tribe of Indians, the Showhegans. They all adopted Indian names, and Ed was appointed the big chief. They even used to tease their sister, Grace, by telling her that they had "Showhegan blood."[8] Ernest himself would claim to be one-eighth Indian and speak in what he called his "Choctaw Lingo," a "joke Indian language" that Lillian Ross made great use of in her "profile" for the *New Yorker*.[9] As a child, Ernest's first doll was a rubber papoose, his second a white Eskimo. He also wore an Indian suit with fringed leggings and loved to enact passages from his favorite poem, *Hiawatha*.[10]

Moreover, the influence of the Indians can be seen even in Hemingway's earliest writing. In a letter to Emily Goettsman, mailed on July 15, 1916, he wrote, "My old Ojibwa Pal and wood-craft teacher, Billy Gilbert, was over to see me Sunday. Billy relapsed into a state of matrimony three years ago. The last time I saw him he was a part of the forest, one of the last of the old woods Indians. Now he lives in a cabin and raises vegetables and cuts cord wood."[11] In this letter, Hemingway cited a passage from *The Jungle Book* that he applied to Billy. Like Kipling's character Mowgli, who leaves the jungle to get married, Billy was "heartsick for the jungle's sake." Though Billy was a part of the forest, he became domesticated because his woman "no like the woods." Even as a boy, Hemingway displayed admiration for the old ways and a sense of regret that times were changing.

Hemingway's first stories would also feature Indian characters and settings. Two notable examples are "The Judgment of Manitou" and "Sepi Jingan," stories written for *Tabula*, his high school's literary magazine. "Sepi Jingan" contains the first reference to an Indian killed on the tracks of the Pere Marquette train. In that work, Paul Black Bird is remembered as "the new fellow who got drunk last fourth of July and went to sleep on the Pere Marquette tracks." Billy Tabeshaw reveals that it was his dog, Sepi Jingan, who really killed Paul Black Bird. Billy left his body on the train tracks, and "the Pere Marquette Resort Limited removed all the traces." Billy concludes, "So when you said that Paul Black Bird was drunk and lay down on the Pere Marquette tracks you weren't quite right."[12]

The existence of an Indian who died on the railroad tracks while asleep has never been conclusively proven. Constance Cappel Montgomery claims that the victim was the father of Tommy Mitchell, a friend of Ernest's and a character in "The Light of the World." According to Montgomery, such deaths were frequent in the Indian camp; one family allegedly had three sons die in this way. Carlos Baker identifies the victim as "a very tall Indian who had given Ernest a canoe paddle made from ashwood." Donald St. John speculates that the man could be Richard Boulton, for his neighbors claimed that he vanished one night and was never heard from again.[13]

Reference to this legendary Indian can also be found in a fragment entitled "No Worse Than a Bad Cold."[14] The genesis for this piece may have been the outdoor productions of *Hiawatha* that the Hemingways would see every year. His sister Madelaine remembered how the family would go to Wa-ya-ga-mung, where they would sit on bleachers facing a small lake and watch the "magical enactment of *Hiawatha*."[15] They were especially enchanted by the young Indian who dove from the high man-made cliff and later sailed off into the sunset. Hemingway's drama is, according to his introduction, an "Indian Passion Play" held at the town of "Wa ga ga wug in Michigan." Although it opens with Longfellow's refrain, "By the shores of Gitchy Goomie—by the shining big sea water," none of the sentimentality of *Hiawatha* is apparent in this piece.

The play consists of two characters, "Paw Paw" Kewis and Dick Boulton, talking and drinking. Paw Paw claims, "Red Man always bitched. Redman on the bum. Redman don't last long." Paw Paw mentions that there is a little girl outside and asks Dick, "What you do with her?" Dick says "Nothing," explaining, "She's a good kid," and he doesn't want to "get mixed up with her." Paw Paw replies, "Ain't any mixed up with Indians. Fuck um say goodbye, you never see em again." The two men then begin to drink "Old Grand-dad-Dollar whisky" which Paw Paw says is the "Great spirit all right. Only spirit I ever seen. Great spirit of the Red Man." Paw Paw expounds upon the liquor's power to make "the water run up hill" and "bring back the wild pigeon." A crossed-out line reads that the Great Spirit also "Brings back all the trees they cut down," which suggests that only alcohol can repair the damage incurred by the loss of the forest and the wilderness traditions. Yet Paw Paw notes the destructiveness of alcohol, claiming that it "makes the red man lie down on the railroad track—only train that take him to the happy hunting grounds." Paw Paw concludes, "Finally every Indian live alone and talk to himself—when he hears enough from himself he go lay down on the railroad track."

A similar account can be found in the fragment posthumously entitled "The Indians Moved Away."[16] In that work, the narrator remembers the smell that remained in Grandpa Bacon's shack long after the Indians moved away:

> Grandpa Bacon could never rent the shack to white people after that and no more Indians rented it because the Indian who had lived there had gone into Petoskey to get drunk on the Fourth of July and, coming back, had lain down to go to sleep on the Pere Marquette railway tracks and had been run over by the midnight train. He was a very tall Indian and had made Nick an ash canoe paddle. He had lived alone in the shack and drank pain killer and walked through the woods alone at night. Many Indians were that way.
>
> There were no successful Indians.

This fragment is the clearest account of the Indian in all of Hemingway's works. It is likely that Carlos Baker gained his information about the identity of the dead Indian from this fragment, given that he presents as fact some of the material contained in this work.[17]

Hemingway would use many of the details of this fragment in his story "Fathers and Sons." In particular, the enduring smell of the Indians is a common feature of both texts.[18] In "Fathers and Sons," Nicholas Adams remembers, "When you go in a place where Indians have lived you smell them gone and all the empty pain killer bottles and the flies that buzz do not kill the sweat-grass smell, the smoke smell and that other like a fresh cased marten skin. Nor any jokes about them nor old squaws take that away. Nor the sweet sick smell they get to have. Nor what they did finally. It wasn't how they ended. They all ended the same. Long time ago good. Now no good" (376). Though in this passage Hemingway never explicitly states "what they did finally," it can be inferred that they all were defeated in some way.

The tragedies that befell the woods Indians are the unstated background, a "thing left out," of "Ten Indians." That Hemingway once called this text "After the Fourth" is significant, for even in his earliest attempts at fiction, Hemingway connects July 4 with "what they did finally."[19] In choosing that fateful date for "Ten Indians," Hemingway evoked the past associations he had made regarding the Independence Days of his youth, invariably connected to the death of the Indian on the Pere Marquette tracks. Regardless of whether this event was fact or fantasy, the death of the Indian on the train tracks affected Hemingway throughout his life. Perhaps the accident suggested that the destructive force of civilization was literally running over Indians in its path. The Indian's death could have served as a metaphor for the high price Indians paid as their way of life was destroyed. Whatever its meaning, the specter of the dead Indian is present in many of Hemingway's works.

In the exposition of "Ten Indians," nine Indians are counted lying drunk in the road from Petoskey. One Indian was blocking the path, and Joe Garner had to drag him out of the way. This Indian, like the Indian who died on the Pere Marquette train tracks, had too much to drink and chose a dangerous place to sleep off the alcohol's effects. Carl wonders whether the Indian is Billy Tabeshaw because "his pants looked mighty like Billy" (253).[20] But he is told that "all Indians wear the same kind of pants" (253). Constance Montgomery reported that Joe Bacon remembered one night when he and his family were returning home in the "big wagon." They passed a squaw who was "dead drunk and lying in the middle of the road." Mrs. Bacon said, "Just run her over, she ain't worth nothing no how." But Joe Bacon stopped the wagon and lifted the Indian woman to the side of the road.[21] Although Joe Bacon did not mention that Ernest accompanied them on this trip, it is possible that he had heard the story because the exposition of "Ten Indians" is similar to Bacon's account.

In the first draft of "Ten Indians," Nick not only sees the Indians passed out on the road, he also sees them in town, surreptitiously drinking beneath the shade trees. The narrator observes, "You did not see that they were getting drunk. They were quiet; they walked along the streets; they sat in the park under the weeping birches and they were seen going in and out of places." Hemingway wrote, "Nick did not see them getting drunk but in the evening they were drunk and Nick saw them, as he drove along the road out of town." Nick is described as "very tired and yet not sleepy but seeing everything for the first time." Nick is beginning to see for the first time what is really going on at the July 4 celebration, just as he will discover the disappointing truth about his relationship with Prudence.[22]

The published version deals only with the aftermath of the celebration. Riding home in the Garners' wagon, Nick becomes aware of their contempt for "Them Indians," as Mrs. Garner calls them (253). Their prejudices are best evidenced in their comments about the Indians' smell. When Nick says, "I guess I know skunks," his friend Carl responds, "You ought to. . . . You got an Indian girl. . . . They smell about the same" (254). That the father laughs at Carl's comment indicates the degree to which such racism is sanctioned.

The attitude of the white community toward the Native Americans is further revealed in "Ten Indians" as the Garners continue to tease Nick and each other. When one of the Garner boys remarks, "I'll bet Pa wouldn't ever have had a squaw for a girl," Joe responds, "Don't you think it" and warns Nick, "You better watch out to keep Prudence, Nick" (254). Although Joe Garner may believe himself superior to the Indians, he still considers them potential sexual partners, as his comment reveals. He quickly amends his statement after his wife disapproves and says, "Nickie can have Prudence. . . . I got a good girl" (254). When Mrs. Garner jokes, "Carl can't get a girl, . . . not even a squaw" (254), she affirms that the Indian girls are often willing sexual partners when the "good girls" are not. Listening to the Garners, Nick becomes aware of the duplicitous nature of the white male relationship with Indian females and of the community's endorsement of such behavior.

Reminded of the prejudices against the Indians, Nick begins to feel "hollow and happy inside himself to be teased about Prudence Mitchell" (254). He is happy to be in love, but it is not an unqualified happiness. Having internalized the prejudices of the community, he is ashamed of his love for Prudence and even denies his relationship with her, saying "She ain't my girl" (254). Nick is also described as "sitting between the two boys in the dark" (254), a position that suggests both his ignorance about Prudence's infidelity and his ambivalence toward her. He is, in a sense, between two boys, one who is proud of his conquest and one who is embarrassed to have an Indian girlfriend.[23] When Nick learns of Prudence's tryst with Frank Washburn, he believes that the Garners' prejudices against the Indians have been confirmed. Joe Garner's prediction that Nick had better "watch out to keep Prudence" is fulfilled (254). To Nick, Prudence is like the rest of "Them Indians," promiscuous and unworthy of trust. He is becoming aware of the mores of the white community, understanding that a relationship with a "squaw" would not be acceptable.

Dr. Adams, like the Garners, is instrumental in bringing Nick to this awareness. Nick's affair with Prudence, like the big celebration in Petoskey, is but a summertime fling. He must return home, literally and figuratively, where his father is waiting, offering Nick, in the words of Paul Smith, "a good cold supper and some good cold recognition of the way things are."[24] Whether he tells Nick what he saw because he thought Nick should know that his girlfriend was cheating on him or because he does not approve of him having an Indian girlfriend is a matter of speculation. The manner in which Dr. Adams tells Nick what he saw is also questionable. Sheldon Norman Grebstein points out the difficulty of determining whether Dr. Adams's revelation "expresses the father's vengefulness toward his son's choice of friends or an honest attempt to perform his paternal duty."[25] While some critics perceive Dr. Adams as cruel to Nick, others view the father more sympathetically. Dr. Adams is clearly a complex character, neither saint nor sinner, but a father who, despite his limitations, cares for his son.[26]

Learning to accept his father's limitations is as much a part of Nick's maturation as is learning to cope with the loss of Prudence. Nick sees that, unlike Joe Garner, his father is uncomfortable talking about sex. Dr. Adams's choice of the phrase "threshing around" indicates the oblique manner and disgusted tone he uses when talking about such matters.[27] Nick would remember in "Fathers and Sons" that his father was "as sound on those two things [fishing and shooting] as he was unsound on sex" (370). He recalls his father's priggish response, "It is one of the most heinous of crimes," when asked about buggery or mashing (371). The Garners, on the other hand, are not judgmental or indirect when talking about sex.

The absence of Mrs. Adams is conspicuous in this story, especially when contrasted to the warm, maternal presence of Mrs. Garner. Mrs. Garner offers Nick a hot supper and seems to show affection for the boy by calling him "Nickie" and by being considerate of his feelings when her sons are teasing him about his Indian girlfriend. Because Nick's own mother is absent, Dr. Adams assumes her role, feeding Nick leftover chicken and pie. In previous versions of "Ten Indians," the isolation of Dr. Adams is more obvious. In a deleted portion of an earlier manuscript, he lies down "crossways in his double bed to take up as much room as he could. He was a lonely man."[28] Clearly, Dr. Adams, one of the "men without women," has been disappointed in love, much like his son.

That Fourth of July marks an end to Nick's childhood idyll. He has ventured into town and returned home, only to find that he can never go back to the protection of his father, the comfort of his mother, or the innocence of childhood. Even his playground, the wilderness surrounding the cabin, is being destroyed as the land is being clear-cut for lumber. The paradisiacal quality of the forest is noted in "Fathers and Sons," as Nick remembers the place where his sexual education took place: "There was still so much forest then, virgin forest where the trees grew high before there were any branches and you walked on the brown, clean, springy-needled ground with no undergrowth and it was cool on the hottest days . . . with the breeze high in the tops and the cool light that came in patches" (372). Nick mourns the destruction of the woods: "Every year there was less forest and more open, hot, shadeless, weed grown slashing" (372). This special shady spot has been violated by the Indians who felled the trees and "left the logs in the woods to rot, they did not even clear away or burn the tops" (372). As Leslie Fiedler observes, "Everywhere in our classic fiction . . . there is implicit suggestion that the Edenic affair is lived out in a Garden in the process of being destroyed. The sound of axes is heard; the trees fall; the ground is broken for factories and stores; and the reader feels that he is being asked to recreate in fantasy a place to which neither he nor the author can ever return."[29] Nick realizes that he cannot return to the virgin forest, for it has been defiled, literally by the Indian bark-peelers and symbolically by Prudence.

The site in the woods appears to be the same place where Dr. Adams saw Prudence and Frank Washburn "threshing around." Nick wants to know exactly where his father saw them, wondering "Where were they in the woods?" (256). Dr. Adams reveals that they were "up back of camp" (256). Nick seems reluctant to believe that Prudence could be capable of taking Frank to the same special spot where Nick had taken her. When Prudence takes Frank Washburn to her and Nick's special place in the woods, she violates not only his trust but the sanctity of the virgin forest. Prudence and her people have desecrated a place where Nick feels "like the way I ought to feel in church," where "nobody gets in here ever."[30] Saddened that the interlopers have invaded his Eden, Nick, like his Ojibwa friend Billy Gilbert, is "heartsick for the jungle's sake."

Though Nick believes that his heart is broken, the story ends on a peaceful note. The conclusion is the most heavily revised section of the story, suggesting that it was the most difficult for Hemingway to write.[31] He finally settled on ending with an image, the wind blowing in the trees, that serves as a correlative of the boy's feelings. In many ways, the ending of "Ten Indians" brings to mind the conclusions of other Hemingway stories. The wind that rushes in the hemlocks the next morning brings with it a new beginning, just as in "The Three Day Blow." When the wind blows in that story, Nick realizes, "Outside now the Marge business was no longer tragic. It was not even very important. The wind blew everything like that away."[32] Similarly, Prudence's betrayal no longer seems tragic as Nick awakes "with the wind in the hemlock trees outside the cottage and the waves of the lake coming in on the shore" (257).

There are also parallels between the ending of "Indian Camp" and "Ten Indians."[33] Both stories end with peaceful images, and the narrators of both impose an interpretation of Nick's feelings, declaring that Nick "felt quite sure that he would never die."[34] However, the events of that night, an emergency Caesarean and a suicide, were certainly traumatic for Nick. His fatuous belief in his own immortality is incongruent with the horrors he saw. Similarly, the comment that Nick forgot to think about Prudence may be a facile rationalization, not an accurate assessment of his true feelings. Whether Nick's "quick rebounding" is proof that "there is a healthy resilience in Hemingway's hero," as Joseph M. Flora suggests, or whether Nick is indeed wounded by what he has experienced cannot be easily determined.[35] Furthermore, although he may have forgotten to think about Prudence when he woke up, he does remember later that his heart has been broken.

Though Nick's relationship with Prudence, the tenth Indian of the title, is the crux of the story, nine other Indians are also significant. Their importance is easily overlooked, for they are only noted in the beginning of the story. The end of the affair with Prudence coincides with the end of her people's way of life as the country is being "lumbered off."[36] Nick may also realize that just as the Indians let him down, they were betrayed by whites, who gave them the products of civilization, like the railroad and alcohol, that threatened their survival. The drunken Indians lying beside the road on the way home from Petoskey, and especially the Indian who went to sleep on the train tracks, are the casualties testifying to their defeat.

One of the implicit ironies of "Ten Indians" is that the Indians have little cause to celebrate U.S. independence. Yet the Indian and the white communities all gathered in town that day for the festivities. Although whites and Native Americans may have joined together on that day, they return home to totally different worlds. Seeing the drunkards lying in the road causes Nick to confront the tragic circumstances of the Indians' lives. And, when he hears the Garners disparage "Them Indians," he is reminded of their inferior status in the community. Though everyone has been celebrating freedom and equality, Nick learns that the Indians really have neither.

In "Fathers and Sons," Nick reflects upon his father and concludes, "All sentimental people are betrayed many times" (370), and "Ten Indians" is about Nick's own loss of faith. Having witnessed the desperation of the Native Americans, the prejudices of the white community, and the desecration of the woods, Nick can no longer be the sentimental romantic. Betrayed in his idealization of democracy, nature, his father, love, and the Indians, Nick learns many hard lessons on that Fourth of July.

Nick is clearly leaving the world of childhood, a world evoked by the nursery rhyme to which the title alludes, and heading toward adulthood. He has gone into town and returned home, only to find that he cannot return to the protection of his parents or the innocence of childhood, for he has seen the Indians drunk on the road and he has heard about Prudence's infidelity. Though "Ten Indians" is about the beginning of Nick's adulthood, it is also a commemoration of a lost world: of childhood, the wilderness, and the Indian way of life.

NOTES

1. Carlos Baker, *Ernest Hemingway: A Life Story* (New York: Scribners, 1969), 13.

2. Ernest Hemingway, "Ten Indians," in *The Complete Stories of Ernest Hemingway* (New York: Scribners, 1987), 253–57. Subsequent references to this work will be cited parenthetically in the text.

3. Item 202-C, "Ernest Hemingway/Chartres/September 27, 1925," Hemingway Collection, John F. Kennedy Library, Boston. See also Items 728 ("Madrid"), 729 ("A Broken Heart"), and 727 ("Notebook"). Item 730 is an uncorrected, untitled typescript.

4. Mary Welsh Hemingway, *How it Was* (New York: Knopf, 1976), 102; Madelaine Hemingway Miller, *Ernie* (New York: Crown, 1975), 26; Baker, *Ernest Hemingway: A Life Story*, 26; Ernest Hemingway, "Fathers and Sons," in *The Complete Short Stories of Ernest Hemingway*, 375.

5. Paul Smith, "The Tenth Indian and the Thing Left Out," in *Ernest Hemingway: The Writer in Context*, ed. James Nagel (Madison: University of Wisconsin Press, 1984), 68. Smith cites an item in the *Petoskey Evening News* (February 15, 1918) that reports that Richard Castle and "a young Indian girl with whom he had been living" committed suicide that morning by taking strychnine (74).

6. George Plimpton, ed., *Writers at Work: The Paris Review Interviews*, 2d series (New York: Penguin, 1977), 232.

7. Peter Griffin, *Along with Youth* (New York and Oxford: Oxford University Press, 1985), 6.

8. Marcelline Hemingway Sanford, *At the Hemingways: A Family Portrait* (Boston: Little, Brown & Co, 1961), 21–28.

9. Lillian Ross, *Portrait of Hemingway* (New York: Simon & Schuster, 1961), 14.

10. Baker, *Ernest Hemingway: A Life Story*, 4–7.

11. Griffin, *Along with Youth*, 23.

12. Constance Cappel Montgomery, *Hemingway in Michigan* (New York: Fleet, 1966), 50–52.

13. Montgomery, *Hemingway in Michigan*, 53–54; Baker, *Ernest Hemingway: A Life Story*, 13; Donald St. John, "Hemingway and Prudence," *Connecticut Review* 5 (April 1972): 81–82. Regarding the fate of Prudence's father, Peter Griffin claims that "one night in town, Boulton drank whiskey with opium and, back at his shack, lay delirious half under the bed. Summoned by neighbor Joe Bacon, Clarence had pumped Boulton's stomach out. But the next night Boulton went into Charlevoix, drank the same mixture, and died" (*Along with Youth*, 32).

14. Griffin, *Along with Youth*, 27–28.

15. Miller, *Ernie*, 26–27.

16. Ernest Hemingway, "The Indians Moved Away," in *The Nick Adams Stories*, ed. Philip Young (New York: Scribners, 1972), 34–36.

17. Baker, *Ernest Hemingway: A Life Story*, 13.

18. Miller remembered, "We even loved the smell of the Indian camp. The odor of their camping grounds remained in the area for a few years after they had all pulled out" (*Ernie*, 26).

19. Ernest Hemingway to Max Perkins, *Selected Letters, 1917–1961*, ed. Carlos Baker (New York: Scribner's, 1981), 250.

20. See Ernest Hemingway, "The Last Good Country," in *The Complete Short Stories of Ernest Hemingway*, 504–53. After mentioning that she had "too much fun Fourth of July," Mrs. Tabeshaw says that Billy is missing: "I no see him in four weeks now" (522).

21. Montgomery, *Hemingway in Michigan*, 98.

22. Item 202-C, Hemingway collection, John F. Kennedy Library, Boston.

23. In "Fathers and Sons," after Nick and Prudence make love, he is again described as "feeling hollow and happy" (373).

24. Paul Smith, ed., *A Reader's Guide to the Short Stories of Ernest Hemingway* (Boston: G. K. Hall, 1989), 202.

25. Sheldon Norman Grebstein, *Hemingway's Craft* (Carbondale: Southern Illinois University Press, 1973), 108.

26. See Robert E. Fleming, "Hemingway's Dr. Adams—Saint or Sinner?" *Arizona Quarterly* 39 (Summer 1983): 101–10. Fleming's article is an excellent study of the different views of Dr. Adams. His analysis is bolstered by his examination of the earlier manuscripts of "Ten Indians." Fleming concludes, "Dr. Adams, therefore, is not to be perceived as a threatening, antiheroic figure, but neither is he to be interpreted by the unquestioning little boy that Nick Adams was in the earlier stories . . ." (109).

27. See Item 730, Hemingway Collection, John F. Kennedy Library, Boston. In that typescript, Dr. Adams says "thrashing around." Whether Hemingway considered the terms to be interchangeable is an interesting point. Although both words can denote flailing or violent movements, *threshing*, used primarily in describing the separation of grains from chaff during harvest, may be suggestive of Nick's maturation.

28. Item 729, Hemingway Collection, John F. Kennedy Library, Boston.

29. Leslie Fiedler, *Love and Death in the American Novel* (New York: Criterion Books, 1960), 347. See also Robert W. Lewis, " 'Long Time Ago Good, Now No Good': Hemingway's Indian Stories," *New Critical Approaches to the Short Stories of Ernest Hemingway*, ed. Jackson Benson (Durham, N.C.: Duke University Press, 1990), 200–12.

30. Hemingway, "The Last Good Country," 516.

31. Items 202-C, 727, 728, 729, Hemingway Collection, John F. Kennedy Library, Boston. The "Chartres" version (202-C) ends with Prudence appearing at the Adamses' cabin late at night. She calls Nick outside and tells him that she "won't kiss anybody again." She explains that

she had to come because "they all came back drunk from town." Clearly not a "sentimental midnight meeting," as Baker described it (*Ernest Hemingway: A Life Story*, 169), but a troubling implication of abuse in her family. The "Madrid" versions (728 and 729) contain dialogue between Nick and his father about "how rotten people are" and end with a description of the lonely Dr. Adams in bed. In the "Notebook" version (727), Hemingway tried out many different conclusions. This version contains the first descriptions of the storm brewing outside.

32. Ernest Hemingway, "The Three Day Blow," in *The Complete Short Stories of Ernest Hemingway*, 92.

33. Ernest Hemingway, "Indian Camp," *The Complete Short Stories of Ernest Hemingway*, 67–70.

34. Hemingway, "Indian Camp," 70.

35. Joseph M. Flora, *Hemingway's Nick Adams* (Baton Rouge: Louisiana State University Press, 1982), 51.

36. Hemingway, "The Last Good Country," 522.

ABBY H.P. WERLOCK

Women in the Garden: Hemingway's "Summer People" and "The Last Good Country"

"IT WAS SO EXCITING in that bank vault," reported Philip Young in 1967 about the discovery of two manuscripts by Ernest Hemingway, heretofore "unknown pieces of fiction involving Nick Adams—the first written, 'Summer People,' and the last, 'The Last Good Country.' "[1] However, Young's enthusiasm notwithstanding, nearly three decades have elapsed since the discovery of these Hemingway manuscripts, and curiously little critical attention has focused on either story. And while Susan Beegel has rightly lamented the dearth of contemporary critical commentary on many of Hemingway's short stories, even more unfortunate is the absence of serious scholarly attention—Linda Wagner-Martin being a prominent exception—to the women in the short fiction.[2] At least two of these neglected stories—"Summer People," written in 1926, and "The Last Good Country," begun in 1951 and revised over a period of nearly ten years but never completed—illustrate Hemingway's development as an artist alternately fascinated and repelled by the complexities of women.[3] Moreover, the stories demonstrate Hemingway's lifelong attempt to comprehend his own conflicting feelings about gender and sex.

The aspiring young writer needed an appropriate locale for his early fiction, and, as Michael S. Reynolds points out, Hemingway violated the axiom that "American authors write about their home towns."[4] Unable or unwilling to use Oak Park, Hemingway found a setting for his fiction in Horton Bay, Michigan, and its environs. These locations apparently appealed to him as an unfettered alternative to Oak Park, one where as a youth he had escaped with his friends to be independent, to drink, and to enjoy some measure of sexual and romantic experience. Using that locale in 1921, Hemingway wrote "Up in Michigan," a bleak story of the drunken blacksmith Jim Gilmore's heartless seduction of Liz Coates, a waitress at the inn. He returned to the same setting in 1926 with the writing of "Summer People," another explicitly sexual story that remained unpublished until 1972, when it appeared in *The Nick Adams Stories*. And he returned to Horton Bay yet again some thirty years later in "The Last Good Country," also published in *The Nick Adams Stories*.[5] The edenic possibilities of the Michigan woods seemed, for Hemingway, a metaphor not only for lost innocence but also for his expression of the troubled feelings associated with forbidden sexual experience. The women in these pine and hemlock studded gardens spark the gender musings and anxieties common to Nick Adams in 1956 no less than in 1926.

The Horton Bay of those years and the events of the summers of 1915–21, with their romantic connotations, remained in Hemingway's memory and imagination for nearly forty years. Horton Bay was the setting of Hemingway's romances with Prudence Boulton, Marjorie Bump, and Kate Smith and of his marriage to Hadley Richardson in 1921.[6] In fact, these romances apparently conflated for Hemingway even before he physically distanced himself from them. Both Jeffrey Meyers and Bernice Kert report that Hemingway introduced Hadley to several former girlfriends on the couple's honeymoon to demonstrate, in Meyers's words, "how much they missed him"; Kert notes that "Hadley did not hide her disapproval of Ernest's vanity" as they went "from house to house meeting the young women who had not won the competition."[7] Real life and fiction continued to merge: for example, Liz Coates of "Up in Michigan" is probably based on Pauline Snow, an older waitress Hemingway knew while dating Marjorie

Bump, herself the model for Marge in "The End of Something" and "The Three Day Blow."[8] Trudy Gilby of "Fathers and Sons" is based on Prudence Boulton, a young Native American with whom Hemingway claimed to have had an affair.[9]

Hemingway's fictive Horton Bay, redolent with sensual water imagery, ripe cornfields, dark cool plantations of pine and hemlock trees, and lush apple orchards, becomes a romantic, even paradisiacal place for trysting, for tasting the forbidden, and for shaping the character of the young Nick Adams, aspiring writer. Just as important, however, it introduces young women not only crucial to Nick's education but stoic, intelligent, and independent in their own right.

Kate of "Summer People" is directly drawn from Hemingway's friend Kate Smith, later Kate Dos Passos. He did not bother to change either her name or those of any of the other characters; the story remained unpublished until after both their deaths. As all Hemingway's biographers remark, Kate was romantically involved with Hemingway while being courted by Carl Edgar, nicknamed Odgar.[10] "Summer People" opens as Nick Adams gazes into a spring, thinking that submerging himself in its cold water will "fix" him (217). In the next paragraph Nick reveals the nature of his problem: while his friends Bill and the Ghee frolic in the lake, Kate and Odgar sit together on the dock. Nick strongly desires Kate, but not while Odgar, to whom Nick feels superior, remains with her: "Kate wouldn't ever marry Odgar. She wouldn't ever marry anybody that didn't make her. And if they tried to make her she would curl up inside of herself and be hard and slip away. He could make her do it all right. Instead of curling up hard and slipping away she would open out smoothly, relaxing, untightening, easy to hold. Odgar thought it was love that did it" (217). The passage is a curious one. Nick's analysis of Kate as resistant to outside pressure suggests her independence and spirit. Yet at the same time he reveals a supreme self-confidence in his own knowledge of and prowess with women.

To Nick at this stage, technique, not love, is the way to "make her do it." In a consciously repetitive manner that echoes the style of Gertrude Stein, whom Hemingway had met in 1922, four years before writing this story, Nick thinks to himself that he knows the secrets of successful seduction.[11] His repetition of the words "making" and "liking" contrast sharply with his avoidance of "loving" at the end of the passage: "It was liking, and liking the body, and introducing the body, and persuading, and taking chances, and never frightening, and assuming about the other person, and always taking never asking, and gentleness and liking, and making liking and happiness, and joking and making people not afraid. And making it all right afterwards. It wasn't loving. Loving was frightening" (218). Here, despite his sexual confidence and bravado, Nick admits his fear of love. Likewise, in his ensuing thought, despite his conviction that he will become "a great writer," Nick admits he does not yet "know enough" (219); he believes such knowledge will be incomplete until age fifty. The repetition of various forms of the verb "to know" in this passage suggests knowing in the sexual as well as the rational sense. Hemingway continues to show Nick's near-admissions of inadequacy juxtaposed to his willed sense of superiority. In addition to the repeated use of the word "know" is the repeated use of the word "it" and other vague pronouns, replete with adolescent sexual connotations. Nick decides to plunge into the lake, where he revels in being "underwater" (220). In an explicitly sexual reverie, he fantasizes about making love underwater: "A girl couldn't go through with it, she'd swallow water, it would drown Kate, Kate wasn't really any good underwater, he wished there was a girl like that, maybe he'd get a girl like that, probably never, there wasn't anybody but him that was that way underwater" (222).

In a lengthy exchange among Kate, Odgar, and Nick, Hemingway expands the water imagery to convey themes that would characterize his fiction throughout his career. That Hemingway closely identified with the fictional Nick is underscored in his repeated use of the name "Wemedge"—Hemingway's own high school nickname—as an alternative name for Nick.[12] Nick wishes he were a fish, announces there will be no 'Mrs. Wemedge," and declares he will "marry a mermaid" (223). Thus Nick demonstrates his—and Hemingway's—conflicting attraction to and wariness of sex, women, and marriage. He also illustrates Hemingway's well-known tendency to depict, in Meyers's words, "his unconsummated love affairs . . . as if they had actually taken place."[13]

During this exchange, Nick lies on the dock next to Kate, who rests her legs on his back and presses her feet against him (222–23). Nick addresses her as "Butstein," the nickname Hemingway gave to the real Kate Smith.[14] The nickname implies a link with yet another of Hemingway's high school nicknames, Hemingstein, the names thereby suggestively blending the woman with the man.[15] In a further indication of this gender crossing, Kate says, "I'd like to be Wemedge" (222). Although it appears here only in embryonic form, Hemingway was to continue this practice of mixing his own name (and those of his male characters) with the names of female sexual partners—particularly, of course, in *The Garden of Eden*—focusing with increasing intensity on androgynous connections between women and men.

Later that night as the group disperses, Kate whispers to Nick that she will meet him in an hour. Walking through an orchard, Nick deliberately pulls an apple from an overhanging tree and sucks "the acid juice from the bite" (224), metaphorically preparing for his imminent rendezvous with Kate. Hemingway not only reverses traditional mythical roles as Nick, Eve-like, tastes the apple, but he also suggests the bitter, venomous, serpent-like nature of the apple itself as Nick willingly sucks the poison from the bite. He then meets Kate in the woods, where, beneath a hemlock tree, they make love. The studied references to hemlocks (and other evergreens, such as pine and balsam), and their association with the act of love was to become a hallmark of Hemingway's fiction. Reynolds has eloquently elaborated on the implications of these frequent hemlock images:

Nicholas Adams and Kate, making love beneath the stars, join a long list of Hemingway lovers whom necessity or choice put to bed upon the good earth. Nick's earliest sexual memory is of Trudy Gilby, the Indian girl who "did first what no one has done better" beneath another hemlock tree. Liz Coates loses her virginity to the blacksmith, Jim Gilmore, at night beside the Horton Bay warehouse: "The hemlock planks of the dock were hard and splintery and cold." Beneath or upon the hemlock tree, his lovers find life. In the midst of the Spanish Civil War, Robert Jordan and Maria make love in a mountain meadow of heather, "and he felt the earth move out and away from under him." Later Maria comes to his sleeping bag laid out on a bower of fresh-cut spruce, "making an alliance against death with him." What our first parents found in that farthest Garden, Hemingway's lovers rediscover: sex and death.[16]

In this early story, Kate, unlike the hapless Liz Coates of "Up in Michigan," enjoys the lovemaking.[17] "Is it fun?" Nick asks. And she replies, "Oh, Wemedge. I've wanted it so. I've needed it so. . . . I love it. I love it. . . . Oh come, Wemedge. Please come. . . . Please, please." Here is the modern woman, unabashedly expressing her pleasure in the sexual act. But Hemingway appears briefly to undercut Kate when she asks afterwards, "Was I bad, Wemedge?"

> "No, you were very good," Nick said. His mind was working very hard and clear. He saw everything very sharp and clear. "I'm hungry," he said.
> "I wish we could sleep here all night." Kate cuddled against him.
> "It would be swell," Nick said. "But we can't. You've got to get back to the house."
> "I don't want to go," Kate said. (227)

In the aftermath of their lovemaking, Nick appears cold and unfeeling. His "technique" extends no further than the immediate gratification of their mutual physical needs. Violating even his own creed, he fails to "make it all right afterwards." Instead, he tells her that she, like himself, must go home, but Kate serenely holds her ground, declaring that she will stay outside all night. As Linda W. Wagner notes, in his early stories "Hemingway was as interested in women characters as he was in men—perhaps more interested."[18] Indeed, at this point the self-assured Nick seems the prude, Kate the liberated modern hero. Kate has a strength and a self-possession from which Nick could learn, but the story offers no evidence of such a lesson. To the contrary, Nick leaves Kate, and the final scene depicts him in bed, thinking "Good in bed, comfortable, happy, fishing tomorrow, he prayed . . . for the family, himself, to be a great writer, Kate, the men, Odgar, for good fishing, poor old Odgar, poor old Odgar. . . . " (228). Kate's name is buried amid the two references to fishing and the three to Odgar. Not only does fishing seem more important than Kate, but "part of Nick's satisfaction clearly derives from the knowledge that Odgar would 'kill himself' if he were to learn of their liaison."[19]

On one level, as the title implies, Kate appears to be one of the "summer people" significant to Nick only as a temporary diversion, a necessary step on his way to acquiring the knowledge essential to being a great writer. But on another, contrary, level she defies definition as mere sexual object: Kate meets Nick at least halfway in initiating the tryst and appears very much aware of herself as a fully sexual being. Furthermore, although the intent of her question "Was I bad?" can be ambiguously viewed as either self-deprecating or generously considerate of Nick, Kate quickly and decisively reasserts herself. It is Nick who, having tasted the apple and known a woman, retreats from this Edenic spot to his conventional bed, Kate who chooses to remain outside, alone, under the hemlocks.

Hemingway's presentation of Kate in "Summer People" illustrates Meyers's observation that Hemingway's fiction usually concerns "one woman in a male world."[20] This strategy is true in numerous works, including *The Sun Also Rises* and *For Whom the Bell Tolls*. However—and here Hemingway seemed uncannily prescient in Nick's comment about a writer gleaning essential knowledge by age fifty—soon after his fiftieth birthday Hemingway began work on "The Last Good Country," a story that contains not one but three strong and self-reliant female characters, including Nick's twelve-year-old sister, Littless; the young unmarried family housekeeper, Suzy; and the middle-aged hotel manager, Mrs.

Packard, all of whom admire and protect the sixteen-year-old Nick Adams.[21]

Understandably, by 1951, the Horton Bay of Hemingway's youth provided a metaphor for childhood innocence quite possibly romanticized by distance and the passing of three decades. Mark Spilka points out that Hemingway laid "The Last Good Country" story aside to complete *The Garden of Eden,* which he had begun in 1946.[22] When he returned to "The Last Good Country," the timing suggests that, on the one hand, having vented his sexual anxieties and agonizings, Hemingway could now celebrate a simpler time by returning to the "last good country" he had known as a young man, bringing it alive through his art. But the timing also suggests that, on the other hand, completion of *The Garden of Eden* did not entirely lay to rest Nick Adams's—and Hemingway's—gender anxieties. In this return to the Edenic setting, Hemingway moves women to center stage. Through a complex aligning of gender roles, Hemingway dramatizes the war between good and evil as Nick and Littless flee to the woods to escape the dangerous world that threatens and pursues them in the form of two men and a boy—the game wardens (the "really bad [but] really smart" Splayzey [105] and the clearly stupid but dogged Evans) and Evans's "no good . . . terrible" nameless boy (106). The combined evil that this trio represents is sharply juxtaposed to the admirable traits of their would-be captive, Nick. His difference from them is explained through the words of women, as in Mrs. Packard's comment: "Nickie, you're a good boy no matter what anybody says" (77). Yet Nick's other, darker side is suggested as well. Nick has a history of losing his temper and reacting to provocation with violence. In fact, Suzy tells Mr. Packard that she is "pretty sure" Littless accompanied Nick "so Nickie wouldn't kill" the Evans boy (107).

"The Last Good Country" opens, like "Summer People," with Nick contemplating a spring. But, unlike the opening of the earlier story, this one shifts the focus in the very first line from Nick to his sister, Littless.[23] Hers is a girl's voice, urgent and insistent: " 'Nickie,' his sister said to him, 'Listen to me, Nickie' " (70).

Hemingway clearly intends to emphasize the sound of her voice, along with the female voices of Mrs. Packard and Suzy, in this story. However, Nick replies to Littless, "I don't want to hear it" (70). On one level, of course, by closing his ears Nick is trying to ward off the consequences of his predicament. On another, though, he truly does not want to listen to his sister: as Wagner points out, F. Scott Fitzgerald, referring to the early short fiction, said in a letter to Hemingway that in those early "stories you were really listening to women—[in *A Farewell to Arms*] you're only listening to yourself."[24] Fitzgerald's words may well have echoed down the years, for in this last story Hemingway appears to have emphatically begun with the voice of the girl and then just as emphatically depicted Nick's resistance to that voice. Littless, the girl at the center of the narrative, is intelligent, courageous, and thoroughly admirable. She, along with the hired girl, Suzy, and the hotel owner's wife, Mrs. Packard, believes in Nick's goodness and provides him with aid and comfort in the face of the "enemy," the two game wardens pursuing Nick for killing a buck out of season.

This shooting of the buck is based on the sixteen-year-old Hemingway's illegal shooting of a blue heron.[25] Although at least one critic finds the change "hard to understand,"[26] a gender-focused reading suggests that by transforming the heron into a specifically male deer, protected by law, Hemingway depicts more explicitly the violation of male codes and male constructs. Nick has broken a male law, and the implication is that the boy must be taught the laws of maleness; until he capitulates, he will be hunted down and, as the text reiterates, probably sent to "reform school" (71, 105). The emphasis on this punishment suggests that Nick must be re-formed or remade in the prevailing image of the males who control the guns, the game, and the women. The game wardens chasing Nick are at once emblematic of the restrictive laws and institutions Hemingway abhorred and of the most egregious of "male" tendencies: their mindless pursuit of the boy who has broken their law, their swaggering, cowardly reliance on guns, and even their drunken, evil-smelling breath are repellent to Suzy, who feels "frightened and disgusted" and who, with Littless, insists on the wardens' lack of intelligence (83, 92).

The exception to these men is the honest John Packard, a principled man set in direct contrast to the game wardens, one of whom, Splayzey, Packard knows murdered an innocent boy years ago in Cheyenne, Wyoming. A man who loves whiskey the way his wife loves culture (99), John Packard looks "more like a peace officer or an honest gambler than a storekeeper" (98), and he tells Nick he must never lie or steal (100).

Mr. Packard is allied with both his wife and Suzy in their common concern for Nick. Suzy, like Littless, uses her considerable wit and resourcefulness to evade the blockades, metaphorical and actual, erected by the wardens. Her defense of Nick is strong and persuasive as she assures Mr. Packard that Nick's killing of the buck was accidental and that it made him feel "awful" (106). Mrs. Packard, too, defends Nick, who demonstrates genuine affection for her. When the "handsome woman" with the "beautiful complexion" (76) bids him farewell, "She smelt wonderful when she kissed him. It was the way the kitchen smelled when they were baking. Mrs. Packard smelled like her kitchen and her kitchen always smelled good" (78). Moreover, although she and her husband are depicted in stereotypically gendered roles, Mrs. Packard apparently enjoys an affectionate, mutually satisfying relationship with Mr. Packard, who "really respected her love of culture because she said she loved it just like he loved good bonded whiskey and she said, 'Packard, you don't have to care about culture. I won't bother you with it. But it makes me feel wonderful' " (99). When he jokingly refers to his wife's hotel patrons as "change-of-lifers," she accepts his teasing: "I don't mind if you call them change-of-lifers," she told him one night in bed. "I had the damn thing but I'm still all the woman you can handle, aren't I?" (99).

Mr. Packard, Mrs. Packard, and Suzy are three "good" characters allied in their loyalty to Nick. However, for all his good-natured relationship with his likable, still sexually active but emphatically middle-aged wife, and despite his reputation as an

upstanding citizen, Mr. Packard is almost imperceptibly but un-
questionably divided from the two women. The fragility of their
alliance emerges over sexual issues and exclusive gender roles.
For example, Mr. Packard and Nick share manly confidences
about sex from which the women are, not surprisingly, excluded.
In one of the deleted portions of the story, Nick assures Mr.
Packard that, in essence, he is normal and red-blooded: "I don't
jerk off," he says, "I fuck."[27] In still another excised passage, Nick
reveals to Mr. Packard that Trudy has departed because she is
pregnant with Nick's child.[28]

These masculine discussions about sex and women are under-
standable when viewed as father-son talks missing from Nick's
life with his own father. More problematical, however, is that Mrs.
Packard, warmly characterized as efficient in the kitchen, "ambi-
tious" in managing the hotel, and sexually exciting in bed, is
nonetheless excluded from the relationship between her husband and Suzy (99). Faint but discernible evidence indicates that
when Suzy worked in Mr. Packard's store, an attraction existed
between the two that prompted Mrs. Packard to ask her husband
to fire the girl (107).[29] And their attraction to each other has not
entirely disappeared: drawn together in the privacy of Packard's
office by their mutual concern that the wardens and the Evans
boy not find Nick, the submerged feelings between Suzy and Mr.
Packard emerge as Suzy prepares to leave:

> "I wish I still worked here, Mr. John."
> "So do I, Suzy. But Mrs. Packard doesn't see it that way."
> "I know," said Suzy. "That's the way everything is." (107)

The gender differences and tensions are implicit among these
lesser-developed characters. Nevertheless, they prepare the way
for the more fully developed and infinitely more complex relationship between Nick and Littless.

Littless volunteers to accompany Nick into the forest. Nick reiterates, both aloud to her and wordlessly to himself, that her
main purpose is to ensure that he kill no one. In this sense she
functions as his conscience, her clear voice reminding him that
killing is wrong. She announces her intention to blend with him,

to become part of him, at the beginning of the story: "I always wanted to be a boy anyway," she declares (72), and in the forest she cuts her hair and practices masculine mannerisms in a way familiar to all Hemingway readers. Nick has taken her to "the last good country" that he knows, and now, as brother and sister lie together in a bed of balsam and hemlock, the scene, seemingly innocent and prelapsarian at this point, certainly sounds a far cry from the sexuality of Nick and Kate or of Robert Jordan and Maria, who lie together to make love amid the hemlocks. Again, on one level, this image suggests chastity, innocent sibling affection, and trust. Not surprisingly, critics have identified Littless with one or both of Hemingway's younger sisters, Sunny and Ursula.[30]

But Hemingway also appears to conflate in Littless a woman from his troubled adult life. Because the last good country is from the outset temporary, a precarious paradise subject to outside invasion at any moment, it resonates with darker implications as well. Nick's sublimated sexuality and implied incestuous longings cannot be ignored. As he tells Littless, he already sees himself as "a morbid writer," one whose stories have been rejected by the *St. Nicholas Magazine* (the pun on Nick's name seems intentional), a children's monthly publication of short stories and poetry (90). Moreover, "The Last Good Country" evokes the title of an earlier Hemingway story, "In Another Country." The source of the phrase is Christopher Marlowe, its implications bleak with the themes of sex and death as well as intonations of male condescension toward women. The full passage reads: "Thou hast committed—fornication: But that was in another country. And besides, the wench is dead."[31]

Hemingway's many liaisons with women, his many fornications, ultimately left him unsatisfied, even his relationship with his last great love, Adriana Ivancich, an Italian woman thirty years his junior.[32] The frustratingly platonic relationship continued for years, and while writing "The Last Good Country" Hemingway constantly wrote letters to Adriana. Meyers, in noting the "unrestrained and passionate expressions of love" in these letters, also observed that Hemingway "again stressed the themes of exchanging identities and merging into a unity when he addressed her as 'Hemingstein' and signed his own letters 'A. Ivancich.' " Adriana was the inspiration not only for *Across the River and Into the Trees* but also for *The Old Man and the Sea* and, according to Meyers, two deleted sections of *Islands in the Stream* and the story "The Good Lion."[33]

No great leap of imagination is therefore required to hypothesize that on that other, darker level, Adriana joined Sunny and Ursula as the inspirations behind the portrait of Littless. Like Adriana, Littless has dark brown hair and brown eyes. Hemingway was so impressed with Adriana's quick intelligence that he called her "fast-brain"[34]; Littless is the literal brains behind Nick's evasion of and escape from the wardens. Fictionally depicted as Renata of *Across the River,* Adriana "had a profile that would break your heart"[35]; Nick gazes longingly on Littless's "high cheekbones and the beautiful line of her head" (119). Hemingway needed Adriana to stave off his solitary bouts with despair, what he called the "Black-Ass" depression,[36] and Nick tells Littless of his "Bad Black lonesome" (84). Furthermore, Littless is sister to Nick Adams, and Adriana—called "daughter" by "Papa"—also appeared sisterlike to Hemingway. Bernice Kert noted that Hemingway's "paternalism [with Adriana] was a convenient mask for some new—and perhaps unwelcome—erotic longings."[37] Because Hemingway identified with Gianfranco, Adriana's brother, Meyers suggests that "Hemingway revealed the incestuous overtones of his emotions. . . . He said to Gianfranco that both of them loved Adriana, but could not marry her."[38] Viewing Adriana as a model for Littless helps to account for the sexually charged, sublimated, and incestuous language in this story.

Adriana's sexual purity was carefully guarded and constantly chaperoned by her mother, who certainly knew of Hemingway's reputation with women. Littless's virginity and innocence are, in the manuscript, juxtaposed with Nick's sexual experience. In an excised passage, Littless asks Nick about Trudy: "You wouldn't go and make her another baby would you?" Nick replies, "I don't know."[39] In the published story, when Littless innocently begs Nick to take her into the forest with him, "She kissed him and held onto him with both her arms. Nick Adams looked at her and tried to think straight. It was difficult. . . . 'I'll take you,' " he says (72). In "Summer People" Nick deliberately eats the apple before his sexual encounter with Kate. In "The Last Good Country," however, he specifically asks Littless to eat it as well (91, 117). Indeed, paralleling, if not undermining, the female voices that defend Nick and declare his goodness is the sinister image of another Nick more closely aligned with the wardens than he would care to admit. Just as Warden Evans sleeps with his ".38 Smith and Wesson" (92), Nick sleeps with his "gun under his left leg" (118). Nick cannot escape the insistent metaphoric presence of his sexuality and the other forms of masculinity so carefully emphasized in "The Last Good Country."

In comparison with the story of thirty years earlier, this one, written by the master of the iceberg technique, resounds with submerged meanings, double entendres, innuendoes. Using such phrases as "come into the swamp with me," (73), Nick guides Littless into the dark forest by "going in the back way" (88). Leading his sister to "a secret place," he takes her to the "virgin timber" where they can be assured of solitude because, as Nick tells Littless, "nobody gets in, ever" (89). In a return to Hemingway's fondness for suggestive vague pronouns, Littless says, "I'm not scared, Nickie. But it makes me feel very strange." He comforts her: "You just enjoy this, Littless. This is good for you" (89). After their difficult walk through the hemlock slashings, Littless, lying with Nick in the hemlock bed and sounding very much like Kate of "Summer People," speaks of the arduous journey and asks, "Did I do all right?" (108).[40]

Telling her that she "did wonderfully" (108), Nick leaves the hemlock bed to fish for trout. His obsession with fishing, as in "Summer People," pours forth here in a burst of old-fashioned Freudian brilliance. Nick's fishing line "straightens" and he feels a "sudden heavy firmness," then a "throbbing and jerking," a "rising" and "a heavy wildness of movement" before the fish subsides, "flopping" on the bank. "He was strong and heavy in Nick's hands. . . . Nick held him in his right hand and he could just reach around him." Nick then says, "He's pretty big. . . . But I've hurt him and I have to kill him." He does so, observing, "He's a perfect size for Mrs. Packard. . . . But he's pretty big for Littless and me. . . . Littless might not like this big one" (110–11). The killing of the fish, clearly in this scene a metaphor for Nick's sexual organ, becomes even more interesting when one considers his earlier killing of the heron, the moose, and the buck; he appears to be attempting to exorcise the sexual drive that has already caused Trudy's pregnancy and that has apparently been aroused again while he and Littless slept together.[41]

Nick then returns to camp only to find Littless transformed. The characteristic use of the word "it" seems unmistakably provocative here:

> "What did you do, you monkey?"
> She turned and looked at him and smiled and shook her head.
> "I cut it off," she said.
> "How?"
> "With a scissors. How do you think?"
> "How did you see to do it?"
> "I just held it out and cut it. It's easy. Do I look like a boy?"
> "Like a wild boy of Borneo."
> "I couldn't cut it like a Sunday-school boy. Does it look too wild?"
> "No."
> "It's very exciting," she said. "Now I'm your sister but I'm a boy, too. Do you think it will change me into a boy?"
> "No."
> "I wish it would." (p. 112)

The few critics who have written on this story do not reach consensus.[42] Yet given the Hemingway of *The Garden of Eden,* it seems improbable that this story is simply an innocent tale of brother-sister affection. Indeed, in 1952, Hemingway wrote Adriana that the story seemed "very simple" but had "an inner complexity."[43] While Littless's innocence seems perfectly genuine, Nick's remains highly problematic. Throughout the story Nick seems torn between two versions of Littless, both of which he loves. The first is the admirable little sister, tough, smart, who "fixed it so you wouldn't get in trouble" (85), who warns him about the wardens, who loves him unconditionally, and who will follow him anywhere. Even when Littless innocently declares she could be his "common-law wife," "Mrs. Nick Adams, Cross Village, Michigan" (121–22), no innuendo is apparent, at least with regard to Littless. But the "Cross Village," as Lynn notes, signals Nick's complex perceptions of their relationship.[44] He vacillates between the boy protective of his sister (118) and the one who secretly watches her sleeping body (119), whose tormented feelings explain the references to *Wuthering Heights*, with its descriptions of the passionate love between Heathcliff and Catherine.[45] By the end of the story, the troubled Nick leaves two possible fates for Littless: on the one hand he realizes he has ruined her day with his dark thoughts and fears, and to atone he promises to take her berry picking. Conversely, in the last lines of the story he promises to read to her from *Wuthering Heights*, that tale of repressed and tormented sibling love that so profoundly moved Hemingway. The story breaks off at this point, leaving Nick and Littless at a literal crossroads.

Among the most provocative speculations regarding Hemingway's reasons for leaving the story unfinished is David R. Johnson's theory about impending rape.[46] Basing his reading on a similar one applied to a Mark Twain fragment in which a young girl would have been raped by Indians, Johnson surmises that, reminiscent of Mark Twain, Hemingway could not bring himself to write of the rape that would be inevitable when the game wardens and Evans's boy discovered Nick and Littless's hiding place.[47] The theory is certainly plausible. Even more likely, however, incest rather than rape was the awful taboo about which Hemingway could not bear to write. Hemingway surely knew the story of incest in his own family tree.[48] With this final story Hemingway found himself, not just his characters, at a crossroads. He could write and had written explicitly about the sexual act, homosexuality, and androgyny, but he evidently could not bring himself to write about incest, the last taboo in this last good country.

Clearly, neither Hemingway's men nor his women can be reduced to simple metaphor. Those strong, self-assured women in Hemingway's own garden could not, in the end, save him from the dark ghosts that haunted him. And, in this last story, they cannot save the troubled Nick Adams. As Wagner observes, Hemingway's men "learn from Hemingway's women. Or, tragically, they fail to learn."[49] But that underlying assumption—that women save men—is itself problematic. The disturbing implication in "The Last Good Country" is that Littless, for all her strength and intelligence, remains—unlike Kate of "Summer People" but like many of her subservient fictional predecessors—dependent on Nick for her education and her self-image.[50] Had Hemingway continued the story, perhaps he intended young Suzy and the mature Mrs. Packard to play larger roles. But, in Beegel's words, both Hemingway's life and the fiction "deliberately resist closure and consensus. Perhaps the best Hemingway criticism should do the same."[51] The enormously strong feelings between women and men, the various crossings of cultural and sexual gender lines, remain unresolved.

NOTES

1. Philip Young, "Posthumous Hemingway, and Nicholas Adams," in Richard Astro and Jackson J. Benson, eds., *Hemingway in Our Time* (Corvallis: Oregon State University Press, 1974), 16.

2. Susan Beegel, ed., *Hemingway's Neglected Short Fiction: New Perspectives* (Ann Arbor: UMI Research Press, 1989), 2–3; Linda W. Wagner [Linda Wagner-Martin], " 'Proud and Friendly and Gently': Women in Hemingway's Early Fiction," in *Ernest Hemingway: The Papers of a Writer*, ed. Bernard Oldsey (New York: Garland Publishing, 1981), 63–71. See also Sandra Whipple Spanier, "Hemingway's 'The Last Good Country' and *The Catcher in the Rye*: More Than a Family Resemblance," *Studies in Short Fiction* (1982): 35–43; and Susan Swartzlander, "Uncle Charles in Michigan," in Beegel, *Hemingway's Neglected Short Fiction*, 31–42.

3. Paul Smith, *A Reader's Guide to the Short Stories of Ernest Hemingway* (Boston: G. K. Hall & Co., 1989), 396, asserts that Hemingway wrote "The Last Good Country" intermittently between April 1952 and July 1958. Cf. Mark Spilka, *Hemingway's Quarrel with Androgyny* (Lincoln: University of Nebraska Press, 1990), 264, which says Hemingway began writing the story in late 1951. Spilka adds in a note that the "original opening paragraph appears on the same page with a roughed out telegram to

Philip Young dated 17 January 1952" (Hemingway Collection, John F. Kennedy Library, Boston, 355S).

4. Michael S. Reynolds, *The Young Hemingway* (New York: Basil Blackwell Ltd., 1986), 52. Numerous critics have speculated on Hemingway's avoidance of Oak Park in his fiction: see, for example, Philip Young, "Big World Out There," in Jackson J. Benson, ed., *The Short Stories of Ernest Hemingway: Critical Essays* (Durham: Duke University Press, 1975), 28–29; and Spilka, *Hemingway's Quarrel*, 196.

5. Ernest Hemingway, "The Last Good Country," in *The Nick Adams Stories* (New York: Charles Scribner's Sons, 1972), 70–132 and "Summer People," in *The Nick Adams Stories*, 217–28. All further references to these stories will be cited parenthetically in the text.

6. Reynolds, *The Young Hemingway*, 248.

7. Jeffrey Meyers, *Hemingway: A Biography* (New York: Harper & Row, 1985), 61; and Bernice Kert, *The Hemingway Women: Those Who Loved Him—the Wives and Others* (New York & London: W. W. Norton & Company, 1983), 103.

8. Reynolds, *The Young Hemingway*, 246.

9. Prudence also appears as Trudy Gilby in "The Last Good Country" and as Prudie Mitchell in "Ten Indians." Speculation abounds about Hemingway's earliest sexual experience: for example, Kenneth S. Lynn, *Hemingway* (New York: Simon & Schuster, 1987), 52, citing Mary Hemingway's assertion, suggests that Hemingway's sexual initiation occurred with Prudence, as does Kert, *The Hemingway Women*, 74; Meyers, *Hemingway: A Biography*, 49, 52, believes Hemingway's first experience involved Pauline Snow.

10. Kate Smith appears in the story as Kate; her brother, Bill, appears as Bill; Carl Edgar, is included as Odgar; and Hemingway's friend Jack Pentecost, known as the Ghee, is the Ghee, in the story (Young, "Big World Out There," 41). No one knows the extent of the relationship between Hemingway and Kate Smith, but no critics have found proof that they were lovers. See, for example, Kert, *The Hemingway Women*, 43, and Meyers, *Hemingway: A Biography*, 217, who believe that the romance remained physically unconsummated.

11. Kert, *The Hemingway Women*, 104.

12. Kert, *The Hemingway Women*, 45.

13. Meyers, *Hemingway: A Biography*, 217.

14. Kert, *The Hemingway Women*, 45.

15. Lynn, *Hemingway*, 59.

16. Reynolds, *The Young Hemingway*, 124.

17. Critics have responded with remarkable divergence to this graphically described love scene. Lynn calls the entire story "repulsive and possibly wish-fulfilling" (*Hemingway*, 128); Reynolds, to the contrary, praises it: "In frank and tender nakedness, they make love. . . . Nick, as explicitly as Hemingway could write at that time, shows a sophisticated technique to

which Kate responds beautifully" (*The Young Hemingway*, 123). Kert, noting the "imprint of boyish fantasy," says that she cannot blame the young virginal Hemingway "for imagining himself a sexual acrobat" (*The Hemingway Women*, 46).

18. Wagner, " 'Proud and Friendly and Gently,' " 66.

19. Lynn, *Hemingway*, 128–29.

20. Meyers, *Hemingway: A Biography*, 319.

21. Nick's mother remains out of sight, confined to her room with a "sick headache." Likewise his father, referred to only once, is apparently away from home. By deliberately moving the parents offstage, Hemingway freed himself to set up and explore nonparental gender alignments.

22. Spilka, *Hemingway's Quarrel*, 277.

23. Spilka notes that Hemingway had initially opened the story in the first person but substituted the lines quoted above, elevating Littless "into special prominence" (*Hemingway's Quarrel*, 267). The next few lines in the published story describe Nick: "He was watching the bottom of the spring where the sand rose in small spurts with the bubbling water" (70). Cf. the opening lines of "Summer People," in which "Nick put his arm down into the spring. . . . He felt the featherings of the sand spouting up from the spring cones at the bottom against his fingers" (217).

24. Quoted in Wagner, " 'Proud and Friendly and Gently,' " 63, from Fitzgerald's letter to Hemingway, Hemingway Collection, John F. Kennedy Library, Boston.

25. Numerous critics have noted the importance of this event in the youthful Hemingway's life. See, for example, Lynn, *Hemingway*, 56, Meyers, *Hemingway: A Biography*, 15, and Spilka, *Hemingway's Quarrel*, 133.

26. Young, "Big World Out There," 36.

27. Second version of "The Last Good Country" in the Hemingway Collection, John F. Kennedy Library, Boston, 84. Quoted in several published sources; see, for example, Spilka, *Hemingway's Quarrel*, 345–46.

28. Again, several critics note the deletion of this information in the published version of the story. See, for example, Smith, *Reader's Guide*, 312.

29. Packard's sexual interest in the young hired girl becomes even more interesting in light of Hemingway's sexual interest in Prudence Boulton, the Indian girl who, according to Paul Smith, "The Tenth Indian and the Thing Left Out," in *Ernest Hemingway: The Writer in Context*, ed. James Nagel (Madison: University of Wisconsin Press, 1984), 199, sometimes performed housekeeping chores for the Hemingway family, suggesting yet another conflation of two young women, real and fictional.

30. Meyers believes Sunny is the model (*Hemingway: A Biography*, 10); Lynn suggests Ursula (*Hemingway*, 56); Spilka sees Littless as a "composite" of both sisters (*Hemingway's Quarrel*, 142–43).

31. Quoted in Meyers, *Hemingway: A Biography*, 198, and Lynn, *Hemingway*, 353, who notes that T. S. Eliot also used Marlowe's lines to pref-

ace his "Portrait of a Lady." See also Smith, "The Tenth Indian," 199, and *Reader's Guide*, 312, which note that "the only thing he ever forgot about [Prudence Boulton]—and which he must have known—is that she committed suicide with her lover in February 1918 when she was sixteen years old."

32. In a 1952 letter to Bernard Berenson, Hemingway recalled his depression of 1925, when, his marriage to Hadley on the rocks, he sent her on a trip so that he could complete *The Sun Also Rises:* she returned and surprised him "in bed with a no good girl" and he "had to get the girl out onto the roof of the saw mill." His point, though, is "I had written too fast and the excitement was all in me and almost nothing in the book. So I fornicate into that terrible, dreadful state of absolute clear-headedness that is non-believer's limbo" (Carlos Baker, ed., *Ernest Hemingway: Selected Letters, 1917–1961* [New York: Charles Scribner's Sons, 1981], 792).

33. Meyers, *Hemingway: A Biography*, 443, 452.

34. Meyers, *Hemingway: A Biography*, 448.

35. Ernest Hemingway, *Across the River and into the Trees* (New York: Scribner Library, 1970), 80; quoted in Kert, *The Hemingway Women*, 444.

36. Meyers, *Hemingway: A Biography*, 510.

37. Kert, *The Hemingway Women*, 442.

38. Meyers, *Hemingway: A Biography*, 443.

39. File 542, Hemingway collection, John F. Kennedy Library; quoted in Smith, *A Reader's Guide*, 312.

40. The few critics who have written about this story point out the similarities between Littless and other fictional Hemingway women, particularly Catherine Barkley of *A Farewell to Arms*. If this latter parallel to the sexually charged relationship holds, the sexual dimension of the relationship between Littless and Nick becomes impossible to ignore.

41. Spilka's comment on Nick's reading of R. D. Blackmoor's *Lorna Doone* seems apt here: the hero of the novel, John Ridd, metaphorically apostrophizes his love, Lorna: "Have I caught you, little fish? Or must all my life be spent in angling after you?" (See Spilka, *Hemingway's Quarrel*, 137; *Lorna Doone*, 189). Spilka then observes that a "close second to Lorna in [John's] strong affections" is his sister, Annie. Furthermore, as Hemingway told Arthur Mizener, he and Ursula slept together when, just home from World War I, Hemingway felt "lonely in the night" (Hemingway to Arthur Mizener, June 2, 1950; quoted in Baker, ed., *Ernest Hemingway: Selected Letters*, 697, Hemingway, 58).

42. For example, Spilka thinks the relationship is entirely innocent (*Hemingway's Quarrel*, 270), whereas Lynn believes that when Littless sits on Nick's lap, he responds with an erection (*Hemingway*, 57). Cf. Smith, *Reader's Guide*, 118, which interprets their relationship as "largely her fantasy, although there are some cuddly moments that make one wince for Nick."

43. Adriana Ivancich to Hemingway, April 24, 1952, in Baker, ed., *Ernest Hemingway: Selected Letters*, 634; quoted in Spilka, *Hemingway's Quarrel*, 264.

44. Lynn, *Hemingway*, 57.

45. In a 1935 *Esquire* article, Hemingway named the books he would most like to "read again for the first time": *Wuthering Heights, Anna Karenina, Far Away and Long Ago,* and *Buddenbrooks* (quoted in Spilka, *Hemingway's Quarrel*, 12).

46. David R. Johnson, " 'The Last Good Country': Again the End of Something," in Jackson J. Benson, ed., *New Critical Approaches to the Short Stories of Ernest Hemingway* (Durham: Duke University Press, 1990), 314–20.

47. Writing of the fragment "Huck and Tom Among the Indians" (in which a young girl would be raped by Indians), Walter Blair speculated, "Almost in spite of itself, the story was moving toward a head-on collision with a deep personal taboo. . . . recounting such an atrocity was unthinkable" (Walter Blair, "Huck and Tom Among the Indians," *Life,* December 20, 1968, 32–50a); quoted in Johnson, " 'The Last Good Country,' " 319.

48. Patricia S. Hemingway, *The Hemingways: Past and Present and Allied Families* (Baltimore: Gateway Press, Inc., 1988), 153, notes the unexplained Hemingway ancestor of Anson Tyler. In a letter to Malcolm Cowley in the late 1940s, Hemingway jokingly suggested that "incest was best." Hemingway to Malcolm Cowley, letter held in private collection.

49. Wagner, " 'Proud and Friendly and Gently,' " 64.

50. Millicent Bell, "*A Farewell to Arms:* Pseudoautobiography and Personal Metaphor," 114, attributes Catherine Barkley's "desire to please" Frederic Henry solely to "male fantasies of the ideal submissive partner." Her analysis of the submissive nature of many of Hemingway's women applies even to the women of this last story. For discussions of submissiveness in Hemingway's women in general, see Meyers, *Hemingway: A Biography*, 318–19, and Spilka, *Hemingway's Quarrel*, 373.

51. Beegel, ed., *Hemingway's Neglected Short Fiction*, 13.

GEORGE MONTEIRO

By the Book:
"Big Two-Hearted River"
and Izaak Walton

Angling doth bodyes exercise.
And maketh soules holy and wise:
By blessed thoughts and meditation:
This, this is Anglers recreation!
—Nagrom Notpoh,
"In Praise of M. Barkers Excellent Book of Angling"

IZAAK WALTON INTENDED to make *The Compleat Angler* a "recreation, of a recreation."[1] This re-creation in words will offer the writer a second form of recreation, following the recreation offered by fishing itself. Indeed, as Walton implies, fishing and writing about fishing constitute intimately related ways of re-creating body and spirit. Such notions linking recreation with re-creation put Ernest Hemingway in camp with Walton, aligning *The Compleat Angler* with seemingly disparate works such as *Death in the Afternoon* (bullfighting and writing), *Green Hills of Africa* (hunting and writing), *The Old Man and the Sea,* "Big Two-Hearted River," *Across the River and Into the Trees* (duck hunting and war memories), *Islands in the Stream* (sub chasing, fishing, and painting), *The Sun Also Rises* (fishing and bullfighting), *To Have and Have Not* (fishing and smuggling), and *A Moveable Feast* (writing and more writing). The anglers are called Nick Adams, Jake Barnes, Santiago, and Harry Morgan; the hunters (and artists), Harry, Thomas Hudson, and Ernest Hemingway; the warrior, Robert

Cantwell. The wedding of contemplation and instruction with the re-creation of a more or less formalized recreational activity describes Walton's work as well as much of Hemingway's.[2] The case in point is the northern Michigan story "Big Two-Hearted River."

Malcolm Cowley, drawing upon Edmund Wilson's insight in a 1940 essay, offered the first major interpretation of Hemingway's fishing story as a postwar parable of trauma. Cowley was followed by Philip Young, who applied his idea that deep-seated memories of a "wound" lay at the heart of Hemingway's truest fiction.[3] From the start Hemingway opposed Young's thesis, and therefore it seems hardly coincidental that shortly after the appearance of Young's study, Hemingway authorized the republication of "Big Two-Hearted River" in *Field and Stream,* "America's Number One Sportsman's Magazine," as it advertised itself. The cover of its May 1954 issue announced publication of "Hemingway's Greatest Trout Fishing Story," and its contents page described it generically as "Fact Fiction."[4] Here was a way, Hemingway might have thought, to counter those critics looking for deep-seated psychological or even pathological meaning in his fishing story. In *Field and Stream* there was no wild talk about traumatic war wounds. Readers of the magazine could read the story simply as the straightforward account of a fishing trip lasting a couple of days and judge it accordingly.

Hemingway's readers never fully accepted the Wilson-Cowley-Young reading of Hemingway's story, but this interpretation did finally make one highly influential convert. After opposing the "wound reading" for years, Hemingway himself finally accepted it. In "The Art of the Short Story" (intended for a new edition of his stories) he said as much, as he did in *A Moveable Feast.*[5] Yet even the author's word cannot always carry the day. In the classroom there is always that ingenuous undergraduate who balks at the wound explanation, objecting that the war cannot have anything to do with Nick Adams's state of mind while fishing because nowhere is the war mentioned in the text. Even that other undergraduate who readily admits that there must be something on Nick's mind stops short of accepting the notion that Nick's concerns must emanate from his war experience.[6]

Not until 1980 did Kenneth Lynn publish his first full-blown attack on the Wilson-Cowley-Young reading.[7] Denying that there is any evidence—explicit or inferential—to indicate that Nick's dis-ease stems from his memories of the war, Lynn reveals that Nick's inner tension emanates from his situation at home. As he sees it, Nick's main quarrel is with his family, especially his mother. In short, he is still something of an adolescent, vexed by problems he is unable to solve or set aside. Lynn, it seemed, refuted the old thesis only to replace it with a new version, trading the war wound for a family wound.[8]

Hemingway wrote "Big Two-Hearted River" in the summer of 1924. To Gertrude Stein and Alice B. Toklas, Hemingway boasted that he had written a story "about 100 pages long" in which "nothing happens."[9] A year later, after reading the story in the magazine *This Quarter,* F. Scott Fitzgerald and Christian Gauss accused Hemingway—"half in fun, half in seriousness"—of " 'having written a story in which nothing happened,' with the result that it was 'lacking in human interest.' "[10] Later, less in fun and more seriously, Fitzgerald described the story as "a picture—sharp, nostalgic, tense" that "develops before your eyes." "When the picture is complete a light seems to snap out, the story is over," he continued, "There is no tail, no sudden change of pace at the end to throw into relief what has gone before."[11] Allen Tate struck much the same note: "Most typical of Mr. Hemingway's precise economical method is the story 'Big Two-Hearted River,' where the time is one evening to the next afternoon and the single character a trout fisherman who makes his camp-fire, sleeps all night, gets up and catches a few trout, then starts home; that is all . . . the most completely realized naturalistic fiction of the age."[12]

Such straightforward readings are not contradicted by what is known of the origins of the story. At the beginning Hemingway hoped to make his fishing story nothing more than the lightly fictionalized account of a trip he had taken with two companions on the Fox River. But this idea did not work out, perhaps, as Michael Reynolds suggests, because it was "too much the straight story about fishing the Fox." He started again, and "this time he took what he knew about the Fox to a river he had not fished. He did not need the other two men, only the river and his invention, Nick Adams."[13] What remained as well, however, was the experience he had mined once before, in a handful of journal pieces on fishing (and, in one case, camping) that he had published in the *Toronto Star* in 1920. In one of those instructional pieces he had written about fishing in the rapids of the Canadian Soo. These rainbow trout "will take a fly but it is rough handling them in that tremendous volume of water on the light tackle a fly fisherman loves. It is dangerous wading in the spots that can be waded too, for a misstep will take the angler over his head in the rapids. A canoe is a necessity to fish the very best water." Here the writer breaks for a new paragraph, to begin again: "Altogether [such fishing] is a rough, tough, mauling game, lacking in the meditative qualities of the Izaak Walton school of angling. What would make a fitting Valhalla for the good fisherman when he dies would be a regular trout river with plenty of rainbow trout in it jumping crazy for the fly."[14] In the story he would call "Big Two-Hearted River," written in a city thousands of miles away from the Upper Peninsula of Michigan, he does not invoke the rapids fishing of the Soo but the "regular trout river" that he knew as the Fox and renamed to give it a more romantic meaning or "because Big Two-Hearted River is poetry."[15] If not Valhalla, Nick's good place for fishing is idyll enough for this earth.

Izaak Walton, writing in the seventeenth century, fishes in the same "regular trout river," whatever name it bears in his narrative. *The Compleat Angler* is seldom featured in Hemingway studies. Yet Walton's popular book, which by 1983 had achieved nearly four hundred editions, reprints, and translations, is an important source for the two-part story with which Hemingway chose to conclude *In Our Time*.[16]

Consideration of just how Walton's book impinged on Hemingway's imagination when writing "Big Two-Hearted River" begins with questions of genre. Praised for its informality, geniality, ingenuousness, *The Compleat Angler* is truly a generic hybrid. Its focus on the sylvan qualities of unspoiled nature has led some readers to call it a pastoral. Its presentation of fishing lore and its description of technique have encouraged others to call it a handbook or guide. Conversely, its employment of two characters (Walton later added a third) has alerted readers to the dramatic quality emanating from extensive dialogue. Interestingly, "Big Two-Hearted River" started out as an account of a fishing trip taken by Hemingway and two of his friends, but in the rewriting Hemingway removed those friends and by doing so eliminated the possibility for dialogue to enhance his solitary fisherman's contemplative monologues. But as Hemingway must have noticed, Walton's book carried a significant subtitle: "or, The Contemplative Man's Recreation."[17] And, indeed, Walton's book is replete with expressed thoughts, sometimes stated in the voice of his principal character, Piscator (his companion is first called Viator and then, in later editions, Venator), sometimes stated directly in the narrative voice, which is indistinguishable from the author's.[18] "To the Reader of this Discourse: But especially, To the honest Angler," Walton says that he "did not undertake to write, or to publish this discourse of *fish* and *fishing,* to please" himself or to "displease others." He could not doubt, moreover, that "some readers may receive so much *profit* or *pleasure,* as if they be not very busie men, may make it not unworthy the time of their perusall."[19] For "the whole discourse is, or rather was, a picture of my own disposition, especially," he acknowledges disarmingly, "in such days and times as I have laid aside business, and gone a fishing."[20] In fact, Walton creates, according to John Cooper, "a world whose very point is the absence of conflict."[21] So, too, would Hemingway's Nick Adams welcome an adventure—a contest—without inner conflict (though it is arguable that he is not always successful). In *The Compleat Angler*'s world, this absence of conflict provides the key to generic lineage. Making perfect sense of the generic hybridization of Walton's book, Cooper locates it in the tradition of the georgic.

A *georgic* is "a transplanted Greek term for 'the facts of farming.' "[22] Down through the centuries the term's definition has become generalized enough to refer to "a didactic poem primarily intended to give directions concerning some skill, art, or science."[23] Or, as Joseph Addison put it in the eighteenth century, "some part of the science of husbandry put into a pleasing dress, and set off with all the beauties and embellishments of poetry."[24] "The central theme of the georgic is the glorification of labor and praise of simple country life," expatiates J. E. Congleton, but "though this didactic intention is primary, the georgic is often filled with descriptions of the phenomena of nature and likely to contain digressions concerning myths, lore, philosophical reflections, etc., which are somehow suggested by the subject matter."[25] Virgil's *Georgics* stands forth as the primary model for myriad imitations in English literature beginning with the Renaissance, peaking in England during the seventeenth and eighteenth centuries with "scores of poems" imitating *Georgics* "in form and content—poems on the art of hunting, fishing, dancing, laughing, preserving health, raising hops, shearing sheep. etc."[26]

England also had various piscatorial georgics. Cooper noted that these fishing georgics had a second predecessor among the ancients in "the fragmentary *Halieuticon* usually ascribed to Ovid [that] may be called a piscatorial georgic, since it is a didactic poem on fish and fishing, with a description, or rather characterization, of various species of fish and, implicitly, a comparison of hunting and fishing."[27] Walton, according to Cooper, worked directly from the georgic tradition, giving it "a form closer to prose fiction than to the traditional georgic poem."[28] In fact, "*The Compleat Angler* is probably the only work in English," he ventured, "that is still read and that teaches a particular skill while associating that skill with a whole cluster of values and emotions."[29]

A quarter of a century ago Cooper suggested in passing that "Big Two-Hearted River" be considered within the tradition of the piscatorial georgic. Obviously familiar with the Wilson-Cowley-Young theory of the war wound, Cooper wrote,

> In Hemingway's "Big Two-Hearted River," a major georgic
> theme is presented against a background of war and disillusion.
> The narrative seems at first to be merely an objective and de-
> tailed account of a man on a fishing trip, with the same close at-
> tention to the use of bait and rod and even the same concern
> with food that are found in the *Angler*. A more profound resem-

blance is revealed, however, by a fuller understanding of Hemingway's story. The hero, Nick Adams, has been wounded physically and spiritually by war and is attempting to find value and stability by means of the careful, almost ritualistic practice of angling. As in Walton, the contrast is made between rural simplicity and honesty and urban decadence, here by Nick Adams' thoughts of his friend and former fishing companion Hopkins who has, in effect, sold himself in a materially advantageous marriage.[30]

Cooper's work overall provides useful clues to any study of the influence of *The Compleat Angler* on Hemingway's work, as does James Burnham's fugitive review of Hemingway's novel *To Have and Have Not* published in an obscure radical journal of the 1930s that called itself "The Monthly Organ of Revolutionary Marxism."[31] This review echoed Izaak Walton's title but never named it or its author and made a valid and—at the time, surely—original point. Burnham affirmed that contrary to the "critical commonplace" that has called Hemingway's work "purely negative," none of his work has been devoid of ideals or values. He found two of those ideals to be foremost: "to fight, in strict accordance with the rules, alone; and to be able to take it." Apparent in the earliest of his short stories, these ideals are "summed up in the figure of the fisherman, who appears and reappears throughout his writing. The fisherman fights the trout alone with the lightest possible rod and the lightest possible line (what heresy it would be to imagine a Hemingway fisherman using a heavy rod and a worm!); and he shows not the smallest trace of emotion at the heavy disappointment which comes to all fishermen." He explained further:

> It sounds rather silly, particularly when the figure of the fisherman is lifted out the admirable prose which describes the stream and the cast and the strike and the sunlight and shadows. But the fisherman is no accident. He undergoes constant metamorphosis. Here he is again as the bullfighter, alone with the bull, executing the delicate steps as prescribed by the immemorial rules, never giving way, allowing the horns just to brush across his belly. Or he searches for big game in Africa—and eternal

woe to the Philistine who would shoot from the auto (even his wife, as in one story, will have to shoot *him*). Sometimes he simply gets beaten unconscious, or shot, or dies, without a murmur. Or he is in a hospital, in terrible and silent pain, recovering from an immeasurably cruel wound or operation. Or he is perhaps a gangster—a movie gangster, really, as the movies have bodied him forth. And like all fishermen, he talks little, and he often kills.[32]

What is incomplete about this Hemingway angler, averred Burnham, is that his ideals, in themselves "not necessarily either despicable or absurd," had been divorced from "an adequate context, from a completing set of values."[33]

The importance of Burnham's review is that in the 1930s he has already discerned that the figure of the fisherman, in all its avatars, stands at the center of Hemingway's essential work. It is there not only in the early story "Big Two-Hearted River," and in the middle-period novel *To Have and Have Not,* but it will be present in any future work. To measure this implied prediction, one need only name *The Old Man and the Sea, Islands in the Stream,* and *The Garden of Eden.*

If Hemingway's anglers owe a general debt to Walton's angler, there is also evidence to indicate that "Big Two-Hearted River" is directly indebted to *The Compleat Angler* for some of its detail. Such indebtedness is always hard to pin down, and, in the case of Walton's book of directions and information and Hemingway's story fraught with matters of technique and instruction, persuasive evidence of influence is at best elusive. But the details of Hemingway's story need to be compared to similar details in Walton's book. On baiting a hook, Walton wrote,

Suppose it be a big Lob-worm, put your hook into him somewhat above the middle, and out again a little below the middle: having so done, draw your worm above the arming of your hook, but note that at the entring of your hook it must not be at the head-end of the worm, but at the tail-end of him, (that the point of your hook may come out toward the head-end) and having drawn him above the arming of your hook, then put the point of your hook into the very head of the worm, till it come near to the place where the point of the hook first came out; and then draw back that part of the worm that was above the shank or arming of your hook, and so fish with it.[34]

When you use a frog for bait, he advised,

Put your hook into his mouth, which you may easily do from the middle of April till August, and then the frogs mouth grows up, and he continues so for at least six months without eating, but is sustained, none but he whose name is Wonderful, knows how; I say, put your hook, I mean the arming wire through his mouth, and out at his gills, and then with a fine needle and silk sow the upper part of his leg with only one stitch to the arming wire of your hook, or tie the frogs leg above the upper joynt to the armed wire; and in so doing, use him as though you loved him, that, harm him as little as you may possibly, that he may live the longer.[35]

Walton also gives directions for gathering bait (grasshoppers); keeping bait (flies) in jars; searching out fish; and hooking, playing, landing, and cleaning them. He talks about taking "good Trout" in holes and the use of "a moveable string"[36]—the word spelled exactly as Hemingway always spelled it, first in letters and in *Across the River and into the Trees,* and, at the end, in *A Moveable Feast.*[37] Walton's aphorism " 'Tis the company and not the charge that makes the feast" would seem nicely apropos to Hemingway's memories of good and bad times in Paris in the 1920s.[38]

But after all what did *The Compleat Angler* provide for Hemingway? Cooper defined Walton's legacy: "Walton's true successors are not so much the Romantic nature poets as those writers who have affirmed the value of action informed by a piety to and a close knowledge of nature. Angling, said Walton, combines both action and contemplation, and it is this combination that it is the special province of the georgic to celebrate."[39] In distinguishing the georgic from the pastoral (which, admittedly, also influenced the *Compleat Angler*), Cooper noticed that while both of these traditions "deal with the country as an ideal that is contrasted with the less attractive actuality of the city," the country in each case is different.[40] "Nature for the georgic poet is not to be passively enjoyed and it is not merely the agreeable setting for equally agreeable activities. It achieves its significance through intellectual and physical activity, Walton's 'action and contemplation.' It is almost an adversary, although the struggle is the good life. A georgic creates an imaginative experience built around instruction in practical activity. It is precisely this core of practical information that is so foreign to the pastoral tradition."[41]

So, while *The Compleat Angler* is a "prose georgic" (as Cooper noted), "Big Two-Hearted River" is, refining further, a fictional georgic, combining action with contemplation.[42] So, too, to some extent is *The Old Man and the Sea*, while *Death in the Afternoon* and *Green Hills of Africa* can be read as prose georgics. Even Hemingway's essay "The Art of the Short Story" harks back to the georgic tradition, with its employment of a strong "teaching" voice before an audience of imagined pupils. Such heuristic dialogue (between Santiago and the boy, Manolo, between the author and the old woman in the book on bullfighting, between Hemingway and various others in the African book) recalls the dialogue carried on by Piscator, the teacher, and Venator, the pupil, in *The Compleat Angler*.[43] Hemingway was perfectly aware of Walton's book as a teaching text, for he called "Out in the Stream: A Cuban Letter" "one of those contemplative pieces of the sort that Izaak Walton used to write," even taking the name Walton gave his fisherman: "Piscator can see . . . great blue pectorals widespread like the wings of some huge, underwater bird, and the stripes around him like purple bands around a brown barrel, and then the sudden upthrust waggle of a bill. He can see the marlin's mouth open as the bill comes out of the water and see him slice off to the side and go down with the bait, sometimes to swim deep down with the boat so that the line seems slack and Piscator cannot come up against him solidly to hook him."[44]

In this piece, as well as the 1920 piece on fishing for rainbow trout, Hemingway deprecated—but only tongue-in-cheek—"the meditative qualities of the Izaak Walton school of angling." The first manuscript of "Big Two-Hearted River" contained a nine-page coda on writers, writing, and friends that Hemingway later excised. Gertrude Stein's observation that remarks were not literature would have been enough to get those pages scrapped, but there is little doubt that he removed those pages from the story because Stein's reading of the story basically corroborated his own.[45]

Yet from that rejected fragment "On Writing" in the volume entitled *The Nick Adams Stories,* there are things to retrieve. These pages, which would not have been at all out of place in work truly in the georgic tradition, contain some inferential links to Walton's work. Nick talks about "the books" he read in "the old days" that said that the "only way" to fish for trout was upstream, although if you fished upstream "in a stream like the Black or this [the Big Two-Hearted River] you had to wallow against the current and in a deep place the water piled up on you." It was "no fun." Oddly enough, although Walton has been dismissed as no true trout fisherman for doing so, he does suggest (following the lead of Thomas Barker's *Barker's Delight,* one of his sources) that anglers should fish downstream.[46] "Now you must be sure not to cumber your self with too long a Line, as most do: and before you begin to Angle, cast to have the wind on your back, and the Sun (if it shines) to be before you, and to fish down the stream; and carry the point or top of your Rod downward; by which means the shadow of your self, and Rod too will be the least offensive to the Fish, for the sight of any shade amazes the fish, and spoils your sport, of which you must take a great care."[47] This "advice to fish downstream"—Cooper calls "notorious"—runs counter, according to that modern compleat angler Nicholas Adams, to both ease and comfort.[48]

One important anecdote survived Stein's advice. Nick recalls his old companion, Hopkins, whose dedication to fishing was immediately compromised when he learned that his first well had come in. Hemingway might have retained this passage, however, to support one of Walton's strongly expressed principles:

You know Gentlemen, 'tis an easie thing to scoff at any Art or Recreation; a little *wit* mixt with ill nature, confidence and *malice*

will do it. . . . And for you that have heard many grave serious
men pity Anglers; let me tell you Sir, there be many men that
are by others taken to be serious and grave men, which we con-
temn [sic] and pity. Men that are taken to be grave, because Nature hath made them of a sowre complexion, money-getting
men, men that spend all their time first in getting, and next in
anxious care to keep it; men that are condemned to be rich, and
then always busie or discontented: for these poor-rich-men, we
Anglers pity them perfectly, and stand in no need to borrow
their thoughts to think our selves so happy. No, no, Sir, we enjoy
a contentedness above the reach of such dispositions.[49]

Hopkins did not come back even though he had promised to
return the next summer to fish, buy a yacht, and take the group
sailing along the north shore of Lake Superior: "They never saw
Hopkins again."[50]

In the passage from *The Compleat Angler,* Walton refers to "Art
or Recreation." This recalls the notion with which he opened his
book: in writing his book, he "made a recreation, of a recreation." In "Big Two-Hearted River," Hemingway has also made a
"recreation, of a recreation." The story re-creates, in narrative
form, the enacted fishing trip in which Nick Adams obviously
intends to "re-create" himself. If Nick does not directly reveal why
he needs to "re-create" himself (and the narrator also does not
explain), the reader retains the recreation of a camping and
fishing trip in which Nick searches for and regains "all the old
feeling"—"Nick's heart tightened as the trout moved." This response is the ideal manifestation of all the kinetic pressures that
striate the narrative, beginning with the first sighting of a trout,
where the "shadow seemed to float down the stream with the
current, unresisting, to his post under the bridge, where he tightened, facing up into the current."[51] These tensions and pressures
serve to quicken Nick's spirit.

But "Big Two-Hearted River" is also a teaching text. Replicat-
ing *The Compleat Angler,* it offers instruction all the way from se-
curing bait and baiting a hook to eviscerating the catch. In this
story, "there are in effect two parallel processes of education oc-

curring," as Cooper wrote of *The Compleat Angler,* "the dramatically presented pastoral experience and the instruction in georgic skills and georgic values."[52] Nick Adams is Hemingway's modern version of a georgic poet discoursing to himself about the knowledge and practice of fishing and the values of pastoralism, even as, in *The Compleat Angler,* Walton's Piscator is "a georgic poet discoursing in a pastoral setting," laying out a "long and careful exposition of practical knowledge and the related georgic themes."[53] It may even be, as has been suggested, that "the real source of dramatic interest in *The Compleat Angler* is the process or experience of conversion and education that Venator undergoes through his conversation with Piscator. The *Angler* is more than a handbook of fishing largely because it conveys not simply a certain amount of information on the subject but also the experience of acquiring the information and the whole moral vision that accompanies it."[54] Not a bad description, all in all, of "Big Two-Hearted River."

NOTES

1. Izaak Walton, *The Compleat Angler 1653–1676,* ed. Jonquil Brevan (Oxford: Clarendon Press, 1983), 59.

2. Izaak Walton's name has seldom been paired with Hemingway's. When Carlos Baker did so in 1952, he wrote only, "If we read the river-story singly, looking merely at what it says, there is probably no more effective account of euphoria in the language, even when one takes comparative account of *The Compleat Angler,* Hazlitt on the pleasures of hiking, Keats on the autumn harvest, Thoreau on the Merrimack, Belloc on 'The Mowing of a Field,' or Frost on 'Hyla Brook.' It tells with great simplicity of a lone fisherman's expedition after trout" (*Hemingway: The Writer as Artist,* 4th ed. [Princeton: Princeton University Press, 1972], 125). But, of course, Baker did not read the story "singly," any more than he looked further into *The Compleat Angler*'s relevance to "Big Two-Hearted River." Even Gregory S. Sojka, who focuses on the figure of the angler, makes only three or four fleeting references to Walton in *Ernest Hemingway: The Angler as Artist* (New York: Peter Lang, 1985). Gary Brenner, on the other hand, suggests that Walton was a (silent) influence on *Death in the Afternoon,* although he does not extend his thesis to any other Hemingway work. His failure to do so is explained perhaps by a footnote: "Fatal though it may be to my argument in the following few pages, I, well, take the bull by the horns here to admit that none of the existing records of Hemingway's reading or libraries has turned up a copy of Walton's *Compleat Angler.* I find it hard to believe, however, that

he had not encountered it at one time or another. And the resemblances that I discuss seem to me to be too strong for them to be merely coincidental." See *Concealments in Hemingway's Works* (Columbus: Ohio State University Press, 1983), 4, 65–70, 247n. Brenner does not mention that Hemingway refers to Walton and his book in two pieces of journalism, "The Best Rainbow Trout Fishing," *Toronto Star Weekly* (August 28, 1920); reprinted in *Dateline: Toronto: The Complete Toronto Star Dispatches, 1920–1924*, ed. William White (New York: Scribners, 1985), 50–52; and "Out in the Stream: A Cuban Letter," *Esquire*, August 1934, 19, 156, 158; reprinted in *By-line: Ernest Hemingway*, ed. William White (New York: Scribners, 1967), 172–78.

3. Edmund Wilson, "Ernest Hemingway: Bourdon Gauge of Morale," *Atlantic Monthly*, July 1939, 36–46; Malcolm Cowley, introduction to the Viking Portable Library *Hemingway* (New York: Viking, 1944), vii–xxiv; and Philip Young, *Ernest Hemingway* (New York: Rinehart, 1952), 15–20.

4. Ernest Hemingway, "Big Two-Hearted River," *Field & Stream*, May 1954, 45–48, 96–105.

5. Ernest Hemingway, "The Art of the Short Story," *Paris Review*, Spring 1981, 85–102; and *A Moveable Feast* (New York: Scribners, 1964), 76–77. Scribners gave up the idea for the new story collection, and the essay was not published during his lifetime.

6. This student agrees with Stephen Miko, a "hiker" who asks rhetorically "did anyone ever go on a hiking or fishing trip *not* to escape whatever else his life is?" ("The River, the Iceberg, and the Shit-detector," *Criticism* 33 [Fall 1991]: 513). He also concludes that "the action, especially in part two of the story, can be organized as a series of deliberate 'how to' lessons: how to catch, store, and use grasshoppers for bait; how to make flapjacks, including what tools to use and how to tell when they are done; how to prepare the fly-rod, with special attention to gut leaders; how to carry all that you need to the stream" (521).

7. Kenneth Lynn, "Hemingway's Private War," *Commentary*, July 1981, 24–33; reprinted in Lynn, *The Air-Line to Seattle: Studies in Literary and Historical Writing about America* (Chicago: University of Chicago Press, 1983), 108–31. For Cowley's reply, see "Hemingway's Wound—And Its Consequences for American Literature," *Georgia Review* 38 (Summer 1984): 223–39. See also Sanford Pinsker, "Revisionism with Rancor: The Threat of the Neoconservative Critics," *Georgia Review* 38 (Summer 1984): 255–56; R. W. B. Lewis, "Who's Papa?" *New Republic*, December 2, 1985, 33–34; Lynn, "Hemingway's Wars," *New Republic*, January 20, 1986, 6, 40; "Readers' Forum" (letters from Lynn, Philip Young, and Malcolm Cowley), *Georgia Review* 38 (Fall 1984): 668–72; and Lynn, *Hemingway*, 102–8.

8. Robert Paul Lamb's view of the situation is that "the Young and Lynn interpretations only *seem* incompatible. . . . More interesting are the similarities: both perceive in Hemingway a severe psychological disturbance; both believe that once this problem is recognized and the fiction read in light of it then the meaning of the texts will become clear; and both acknowledge that the fiction, especially this story, is difficult to deci-

pher without searching outside of the text." See "Fishing for Stories: What 'Big Two Hearted River' Is Really About," *Modern Fiction Studies* 32 (Summer 1991): 163n.

9. Carlos Baker, ed., *Ernest Hemingway: Selected Letters 1917–1961*, (New York: Scribners, 1981), 122.

10. Baker, *Hemingway: The Writer as Artist*, 125.

11. F. Scott Fitzgerald, "How to Waste Material, A Note on My Generation," *Bookman* 63 (May 1926): 262–65; reprinted in *Ernest Hemingway: The Critical Reception*, ed. Robert O. Stephens (New York: Burt Franklin, 1977), 17–19.

12. Allen Tate, "Good Prose," *The Nation*, February 10, 1926, 160–62; reprinted in Robert O. Stephens, ed., *Ernest Hemingway: The Critical Reception*, 14.

13. Michael S. Reynolds, *Hemingway: The Paris Years* (Oxford: Basil Blackwell, 1989), 282. See also Constance Cappel Montgomery, *Hemingway in Michigan* (New York: Fleet, 1966), 141–58.

14. Hemingway, "Best Rainbow Trout Fishing," 50.

15. Hemingway, "Art of the Short Story," 88.

16. Jonquil Bevan, preface to Walton, *Compleat Angler*, v.

17. Walton, *Compleat Angler*, 59.

18. Walton borrowed much from *The Arte of Angling*, including, apparently, the two characters, Piscator and Viator. The author of *The Arte of Angling 1577* is unknown (ed. Gerald Eades Bentley, intr. Carl Otto v. Kienbusch [Princeton: Princeton University Library, 1956]).

19. Walton, *Compleat Angler*, 59.

20. Walton, *Compleat Angler*, 170.

21. John R. Cooper, *The Art of the Compleat Angler* (Durham: Duke University Press, 1968), 75–76.

22. Smith Palmer Bovie, introduction to *Virgil's Georgics: A Modern English Verse Translation* (Chicago: University of Chicago Press, 1956), xv.

23. Alex Preminger, Frank J. Warnke, and O. B. Hardison, Jr., eds., *Princeton Encyclopedia of Poetry and Poetics*, Enlarged ed. (Princeton: Princeton University Press, 1974).

24. Joseph Addison, "An Essay on Virgil's Georgics," *Works*, ed. Richard Hurd (London: Henry G. Bohn, 1854–1885), I (1872), 154–55; quoted in Cooper, *Art of the Compleat Angler*, 35.

25. Quoted in Preminger, Warnke, and Hardison, eds., *Princeton Encyclopedia*, 311.

26. Preminger, Warnke, and Hardison, eds., *Princeton Encyclopedia*, 311. In sixteenth-century Italy there were even several poems—readers of "Now I Lay Me" take notice—on the silkworm, which was also the subject of a 1599 poem entitled *The Silkwormes*, the first conscious imitation of Virgil's *Georgics* published in England (Cooper, *Art of the Compleat Angler*, 39–40).

27. Cooper, *Art of the Compleat Angler*, 36–37.

28. Cooper, *Art of the Compleat Angler*, 55.

29. Cooper, *Art of the Compleat Angler*, 55.

30. Cooper, *Art of the Compleat Angler*, 56. Moving beyond the narrowly "piscatorial georgic" to other kinds of prose georgics, Cooper fittingly calls attention to Thoreau's *Walden,* the cetological chapters of *Moby-Dick,* and the hunting lore of William Faulkner's "The Bear." *The Compleat Angler* is one of the major sources for *Walden.*

31. James Burnham, "Incompleat Angler," *New International,* March 1938, 92–93. Burnham later wrote books, including *The Managerial Revolution* and *The Coming Defeat of Communism.* He also founded (and subsequently edited) the *National Review.* Incidentally, this review is not listed in any of the standard Hemingway bibliographies.

32. Burnham, "Incompleat Angler," 92.

33. Burnham, "Incompleat Angler," 93.

34. Walton, *Compleat Angler*, 246.

35. Walton, *Compleat Angler,* 288. In a letter to William Dean Howells, Constance Fenimore Woolson alluded to the same passage in Walton: "I like thy tender, half-relenting way of showing [Mrs. Farrell, a character in Howells's "Private Theatricals"] up, like Izaak putting the frog on the hook 'as if you loved him.' " See Howells, *Selected Letters of W. D. Howells,* ed. George Arms and Christoph K. Lohmann (Boston: Twayne, 1979), 2: 110n.

36. Walton, *Compleat Angler,* 355. The author of *A Moveable Feast* (not to mention "Big Two-Hearted River") would not have missed the point of Walton's talk about hunger: "I now remember and find that true which devout *Lessius* says, *That poor men, and those that fast often, have much more pleasure in eating than rich men and gluttons, that always feed before their stomachs are empty of their last meat, and call for more: for by that means they rob themselves of that pleasure that hunger brings to poor men*" (253).

37. It may be worth noting that the *New York Times* has appropriated the spelling Hemingway made famous. For a recent example of its own "moveable feast" advertisement, see the *Times* for July 9, 1993, p. D26.

38. Walton, *Compleat Angler,* 96.

39. Cooper, *Art of the Compleat Angler*, 58.

40. Cooper, *Art of the Compleat Angler,* 59.

41. Cooper, *Art of the Compleat Angler,* 65–66.

42. Cooper, *Art of the Compleat Angler,* 143.

43. Cooper, *Art of the Compleat Angler,* 79. "Piscator must not only teach; he must persuade. He must not only pass on information; he must also communicate the special quality of the information, its dignity, its interest, its total moral and human significance. Much of Piscator's display of bookish learning has this rhetorical function" 156.

44. Hemingway, "Out in the Stream," 173–74.

45. These rejected pages first achieved print as "On Writing," in Hemingway's *The Nick Adams Stories,* preface by Philip Young (New York: Scribners, 1972). B. J. Smith sees in them the explicit evidence supporting her reading that the fishing in "Big Two-Hearted River" carries an ad-

ditional metaphorical meaning in that it is also about writing (" 'Big Two-Hearted River': The Artist and the Art," *Studies in Short Fiction* 20 [Spring-Summer 1983]: 129–32). Lamb's "Fishing for Stories" elaborates extensively on Smith's thesis. For a study of the surviving manuscript at the Humanities Research Center, University of Texas, Austin, see Max Westbrook, "Text, Ritual, and Memory: Hemingway's 'Big Two-Hearted River,' " *North Dakota Quarterly* 60 (Summer 1992): 14–25.

46. Barker advised "You must angle alwayes with the point of the rod down the stream, for trouts have not quickness of sight so perfect up the stream as they have opposite against them" (Thomas Barker, *Barker's Delight: or, The Art of Angling*, 153).

47. Walton, *Compleat Angler*, 255.

48. Cooper, *Art of the Compleat Angler*, 141. The conventional wisdom on the matter of fishing downstream or upstream is displayed in David Foster's *The Scientific Angler: Being a General and Instructive Work on Artistic Angling*: "The rodster should invariably fish up stream, as by that means not only will his bait act as herald in advance, but he has the additional advantage of being able to take note carefully of the particular position tenanted by the fish, and to regulate his cast accordingly" (compiled by his Sons, and edited by Wm. C. Harris [New York: Orange Judd, 1883], 93). Andrew Lang, whose introduction to the Everyman's Library edition of *The Compleat Angler* appears in all seven editions published between 1906 and 1925, wrote: "Both men [Barker and Walton] insist on fishing down stream, which is, of course, the opposite of the true art, for fish lie with their heads up stream, and trout are best approached from behind" (London: J. M. Dent/New York: E. P. Dutton, 1906, xxxii). In Zane Grey's "A Trout Fisherman's Inferno," which begins as a realistic treatment of trout fishing, a solitary fisherman begins "to fish downstream" (his "mind in harmony with the racing current") and hooks a big fish that pulls him further and further downstream until he lands in hell. It is all a dream, of course, but it is as if the angler must pay for this transgression of what Lang calls the "true art" of fishing (*Field and Stream* [April 1910]; reprinted in *Zane Grey: Outdoorsman*, ed. George Reiger [Englewood Cliffs: Prentice-Hall, 1972], 282–91). Hemingway owned several of Grey's fishing books, three of which are now in Cuba at Finca Vigía (see Michael S. Reynolds, *Hemingway's Reading 1910–1940: An Inventory* [Princeton: Princeton University Press, 1981], 132, and James D. Brasch and Joseph Sigman, *Hemingway's Library: A Composite Record* [New York & London: Garland, 1981], 155).

49. Walton, *Compleat Angler*, 176–77.

50. Ernest Hemingway, "Big Two-Hearted River," in *In Our Time* (New York: Scribners, 1930), 191.

51. Hemingway, "Big Two-Hearted River," 178.

52. Cooper, *Art of the Compleat Angler*, 75.

53. Cooper, *Art of the Compleat Angler*, 75.

54. Cooper, *Art of the Compleat Angler*, 122.

Hemingway's Later Work:
A Farewell
to Oak Park

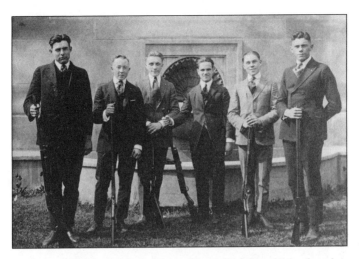

As an editor of the high school newspaper, Ernest (far left) submitted stories about the activities of a mythical group, the Shotgun Club. Near the end of the school year, he gathered several of his friends and posed with them in front of the school. The picture did not appear in the published annual. Published with the permission of The Ernest Hemingway Foundation of Oak Park.

The *Trapeze* staff in 1917. Ernest was a reporter for the high school newspaper for two years; in their senior year, both Ernest and Marcelline were editors of the paper. Marcelline is third from the left, Ernest second from the right, in the front row. Published with the permission of the Oak Park and River Forest High School.

Back in Oak Park in 1919, Ernest wore a leather jacket, a military cap, and the cordovan boots he had bought in New York before going to Italy. Published with the permission of The Ernest Hemingway Foundation of Oak Park.

On February 16, 1919, representatives from the Italian Consulate in Chicago gathered in Grace's music room to celebrate Ernest's return as a war hero. Dr. and Mrs. Hemingway are standing below the Italian Flag draped from the balcony. Ernest is seated directly in front of his mother, Photography by M. O. Granata. Published with the permission of the John F. Kennedy Library, Boston.

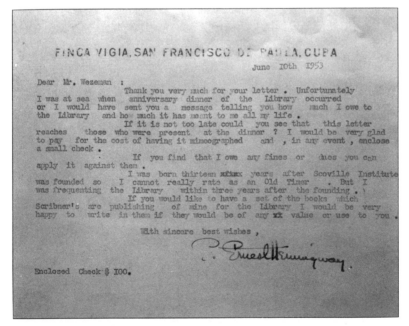

Ernest wrote home to Oak Park in 1953, sending a check for $100, on the occasion of a celebration in honor of the town library. Published with the permission of The Oak Park Public Library.

Afterword

MORRIS BUSKE

What If Ernest Had Been Born on the Other Side of the Street?

MARTHA GELLHORN, Ernest Hemingway's third wife, visited Chicago some years after she and Ernest were divorced. A friend learned that Martha had never been to Oak Park and offered to show her where Hemingway grew up. They drove out and parked across the street from Hemingway's boyhood home at 600 North Kenilworth Avenue. It is a big house, three stories high with eight bedrooms, certainly not the largest in Oak Park but an impressive residence. The two women sat in the car viewing the house in silence for a long minute, and finally Martha spoke: "Son of a bitch," she said, "he told me he grew up in a slum."

The adult Hemingway told a number of fibs about his youth in Oak Park to his wives and to many other people, and he took steps to keep his fabrications from being exposed. It is no secret that he once threatened to stop his monthly support payments to his mother if she did not cancel an interview with a reporter who would question her about her son's early years. Grace gave in to Ernest's demand, and the interview never took place.

Some of the Hemingway myths have rumbled on, often perpetuated by people who know better: by repetition, these stories have taken on the gloss of fact. One of my favorites was told by Hemingway to support his macho image. As an adult he sometimes described the youthful Ernest as a rebel, a perpetual truant on the verge of being sent to reform school. I once encountered an Asiatic echo of the myth. Some years ago a camera crew from South Korea came to Oak Park while making a documentary film on American authors. The woman who acted as translator for the crew asked, "Hemingway left his house twice, no?" Fortunately, I caught her intent, and I asked, "You mean, did he run away from home twice?" She answered "Yes."

This subject had been bandied about for years, and to get at the truth I once asked Ernest's sister Carol specifically whether Ernest had run away from home. Her answer was delightful: she said, "If he had run away from home I think we would have known about it." But the South Korean woman was obviously not convinced by my denial and that of Sue Crist, Ernest's close friend from high school, who was also present. The translator promised to send me a copy of the program she and the film crew produced, but it has not yet arrived. I suspect that television viewers in East Asia, or at least in South Korea, are being informed that Ernest Hemingway left his house twice. Thus Hemingway myths circle the globe and misinform us all.

Superficially, tracking down and vetting Hemingway stories is fun, but there is a serious undercurrent. If we are ever truly to understand the incredibly complex Hemingway, we need first to establish the facts about his life. Accurate conclusions come from accurate data; false data lead to false conclusions. To believe that an adolescent Hemingway sought to escape from a hostile and confining Oak Park environment tells us something about both Hemingway and Oak Park; to learn that he did not try to escape tells us something quite different about them both. The Ernest Hemingway Foundation of Oak Park is uniquely positioned to separate fact from fiction in Hemingway's formative years and to suggest their effect on his development.

As a point of departure it might be useful to consider only one aspect of Hemingway's life in Oak Park: his experiences in the home of his grandfather Hall and their effect upon him. Hemingway was born on July 21, 1899, at 439 North Oak Park Avenue, in the home of his mother's father, Ernest Hall, from whom he inherited his first name. Here he spent his first six years, the most important years of his life, in a home of comparative comfort where the arts and literature were much emphasized. Had he been born across the street, at 444 North Oak Park Avenue, the home of Anson Hemingway, his father's father, the underlying values of his early years would have been very different.

The houses of his two grandfathers were almost directly across the street from each other; both were spacious, and both proclaimed prosperity and stability. A round turret graced the Queen Anne home of Ernest Hall, and the Hemingway house was decorated by a square turret. The lives of Hemingway's grandfathers were also markedly parallel. The two men were born within four years of each other, Ernest Hall in 1840 and Anson Hemingway in 1844. Both were of English ancestry, as were the wives to whom they were happily married, and each survived his wife. Both men were pillars of the Oak Park community, active in their churches, upholders of traditional ethical values and standards of conduct, and both prospered in business, where they were successful salesmen. Hemingway's livelihood came from selling Oak Park real estate; Hall, until he retired, had been a partner in a wholesale cutlery firm in Chicago. Their houses testified to their success and their traditional values, for each man had his house built according to his wishes. The similarity of their homes reflects the similarity of their careers and outlooks.

In religion, both were devout Christians who carried religious observances into their daily lives. Grace was said before meals, and family worship in the home was customary. They were good men, upright, moral, cast in the Victorian mold but admirable by almost any standard in any age. Both men had left farms to serve in the Union army during the Civil War, and both were injured by Confederate projectiles, neither in battle.

There were differences between the two, of course. In religion, Anson Hemingway was a member of the First Congregational Church. Descended from the Puritans, the Congregationalists worshiped a stern, Old Testament God. God's word could be found in Scripture, and in Anson Hemingway's Civil War diaries he speaks often of going alone into the woods on Sundays to read from his Bible and ponder its meaning. After the war, and after he had completed his high school education at the Wheaton Academy and married Adelaide Edmonds, Anson Hemingway became the first general secretary of the Chicago YMCA. His conservative religious views caused him, as a matter of conscience, to oppose those who favored "modernization" of the YMCA. Some of those on the YMCA board, including the son of Cyrus McCormick, the farm-implement manufacturer, urged that they introduce athletic activities, public affairs discussions, and similar nonreligious programs. Hemingway, a friend of Dwight Moody, favored the expansion of evangelistic work instead. Disagreement over policy led Hemingway to resign as secretary in 1883, but he was persuaded to return. As of the end of 1887, however, with the disharmony continuing, he resigned for good after nearly ten years of service, and he went into real estate sales. The years until his death in 1926 were a time of tremendous population growth in Oak Park, with a corresponding rise in property values. Anson Hemingway rode the tide of that prosperity and benefited from it.

In Anson Hemingway's world there were many prohibitions: no smoking, drinking, dancing, or card playing. Ernest Hall's Episcopal church was less restrictive; it held the more traditional, more ceremonious services in richer surroundings that included the display of statues. Hall's view of God was warmer, less intellectual, more personal than that of Hemingway. In a touching scene, Ernest Hemingway's sister Marcelline described her grandfather Hall at daily prayer in his parlor. After reading a selection from *Daily Strength for Daily Needs,* he knelt, not with head bowed, eyes closed, and face solemn but smiling with face and eyes turned upward. In her words, "I liked to watch Abba through my fingers, because he seemed so surely to be talking to his friend God." Ernest Hemingway was present at these daily ceremonies; he could scarcely have been unaffected by them. Throughout his life, he sought to reach the religious certainty that had been achieved by Grandfather Hall.

Ernest Hall's daughter Grace told how on one occasion her father was coming home from Chicago on a streetcar. On impulse, under what he thought to be divine guidance, he left the streetcar, entered a little church, and gave fifty dollars to the astonished minister. The minister had been at prayer, asking for God's help; he needed $50 to keep the church from closing. He was amazed at this providential bounty given by Ernest Hall. I think that Anson Hemingway would have checked into the financial management of a needy church before he gave fifty dollars to it.

Ernest Hall held a more relaxed view of life than did Anson Hemingway; his religion offered greater room for enjoyment. For Anson Hemingway, use of tobacco in any form was anathema; for Hall, smoking a pipe after dinner in the family library with his brother-in-law Tyley Hancock was a pleasant tradition. Marcelline recalled opening the library door a crack to sniff the aroma.

There seems to be little doubt of the artistic ability of Caroline Hall, Ernest's grandmother. She had been in demand as a singer in Chicago and had played both the piano and her melodeon, which survived the Great Chicago Fire. Although she died four years before Ernest was born, her paintings still decorated the house. Perhaps the artwork predisposed Ernest to an interest in the artistic movements he later encountered in Paris, which profoundly influenced his writing.

Music certainly constituted an important part of Ernest's environment in the Hall household. Grace Hall Hemingway dutifully followed her mother's advice to stay out of the kitchen, devoting herself to her music and, in time, to the raising of her children. Grace gave singing lessons even before she and Dr. Hemingway were married, and music was played just for enjoyment by Grace and her family. Ernest Hall's interest in music was as keen as that of his wife or daughter. For many years he held a season ticket to the Chicago opera, seated in the front row beside his friend George Upton, music critic for the *Chicago Tribune*, neither man ever missing a night. And Ernest Hall's ancestral credentials were impeccable. He was descended from Edward Miller, perhaps the leading musicologist of eighteenth-century England, and his son William, a violinist of rare talent.

Quite different influences were at work in the home of Anson Hemingway. Adelaide Hemingway, Ernest's grandmother, was interested not in the arts but in science. She had studied astronomy and botany at Wheaton College and delighted in pointing out to her children and grandchildren the wonders to be seen in the formation of flowers. Marcelline wrote about Adelaide Hemingway's fascinating conversation regarding botany and about how at night her background in astronomy could make the heavens come alive. We can be sure that her love of nature was passed on to Ernest, not only directly through her but through her son, Clarence.

If Ernest had been born in the Hemingway home he would still have felt the artistic and creative interests of his mother, but such influences would not have come from the Hemingways. I have seen no evidence of literary interests (except for religious ones) or encouragement of artistic creativity in the household of Anson Hemingway, with one possible exception: Anson's daughter Grace came to be widely known as a gifted entertainer, a reader of stories for children. Cousin Isabel Hemingway, daughter of Dr. Willoughby Hemingway, and like him a missionary, wrote that she had stayed in Anson Hemingway's home on occasion and that it was a place where "children were to be seen and not heard." Ernest Hall, on the other hand, admired and encouraged Ernest's imagination, predicting that if nothing happened to him the world would hear from him one day.

It is of some interest to find that Ernest's grandfathers differed completely in their view of their military experience in the Civil War. Anson joined the Union Army on July 21, 1862, and served in the infantry and medical departments, mostly on duty in Tennessee and in the area of Vicksburg, Mississippi. Although he was in ill health much of the time, he seems not to have disliked military service. In fact, he stayed in the army until March 7, 1866, nearly a year after the war ended. Back home, he became almost a professional veteran, speaking at Oak Park elementary schools about his war years and enjoying parades and Grand Army of the

Republic outings. Anson ended his service with the rank of lieutenant. Ernest's insistence on being called a lieutenant in the Red Cross (a rank to which he was not entitled) may have stemmed from a wish to equal Anson's rank.

Ernest Hall's military record was quite different. He joined an Iowa cavalry unit on September 21, 1861, and some months later was wounded in the left thigh by a bullet he carried for the rest of his life. The wound caused him to be confined to a hospital during July 1862 and led to his discharge from the cavalry on August 11 of that year, less than eleven months after he enlisted. There was always a cloud over the whole episode of his wounding, not a hint of cowardice but of something being not quite right. As his official record says, rather mysteriously, his wound came "not in the regular discharge of his duties, though from an enemy in arms." Like his grandson, who muffled his youthful record in Oak Park, Ernest Hall kept silent about his military service. In fact, he forbade mention of the Civil War in his house. The Grand Army of the Republic document on his military record noted that an army service was not used at his funeral. It is from Grandfather Hemingway, not Grandfather Hall, that Ernest gained his lifelong fascination with war.

Ernest Hemingway was lucky to have been born in the Hall home and to have spent his first six years there. It was a secure, loving, happy place filled with music and laughter, a wonderful place to grow in every sense. We gain a glimpse of that growth in Ernest Hemingway's first book, which was given to the Ernest Hemingway Foundation by the Sanford family, descendants of Marcelline. Because the book has only recently come to light, and because its contents are so revealing, let us examine it in detail. It is made of sheets of letter paper (8 1/2" × 11") folded to make pages 8 1/2" × 5 1/2". It is validated by the use of Dr. Hemingway's letterhead with the address of Grandfather Hall. The first page reads, in Grace's handwriting, "Ernest Miller made this book all himself illustrated it and named all his drawings at 2 years 7 mo. Mar. 8, 1902."

His drawings, one per page, appear in this order with his mother's notations:

215

"Pipe" [that of his Grandfather Hall?]

"Giraffe" [perhaps as shown in a picture book he had seen?]

"Noah's ark with animals in it" [a reflection of religious training?]

"Sailing in the sea" [a forerunner of his love affair with the Gulf Stream?]

"Man in the moon" [the result of Grandmother Hemingway's talks on astronomy?]

"Bow and arrow" [an indication that he had seen his father's collection of Indian artifacts?]

"2 guns" [relating to his having first fired a rifle only a month before?]

This book wonderfully reveals the past (the teaching, materials, and experiences that had been offered to Ernest and his response to them) and the future (the fascination even at two years and seven months with books and the relationship of ideas and words and images that would illuminate his life's work).

Grace makes no mention of her father's death in the memory books in which she recorded Ernest's growth, but there is a biographical sketch of Ernest Hall. Grace's final comment about her father is that "he was almost as familiar with pictures and artists as with music and musicians, and passionately loved both forms of art." After a lingering illness, Ernest Hall died on May 10, 1905, of Bright's disease. Ernest Hemingway had lived in his home for six years and nearly two months. Grace's memory book carries a picture of the parlor at 439 North Oak Park Avenue that Ernest now would leave forever. If he had lived in the house across the street, he would have received the scientific training of the Hemingway family, but not the same warmth, love, and artistic influence of his grandfather Hall.

Bibliography

Addison, Joseph. "An Essay on Virgil's Georgics." In *The Works of Joseph Addison*, ed. Richard Hurd, vol. 1. London: Henry G. Bohn, 1854–85.

Allen, James Lane. *Aftermath: Part Second of "A Kentucky Cardinal."* New York: Harper, 1896.

————. *A Kentucky Cardinal: A Story*. New York: Harper, 1985.

The Arte of Angling 1577. Ed. Gerald Eades Bentley. Princeton: Princeton University Library, 1956.

Baker, Carlos. *Ernest Hemingway: A Life Story*. New York: Scribners, 1969.

————. *Hemingway: The Writer as Artist*. 4th ed. Princeton: Princeton University Press, 1972.

————, ed. *Ernest Hemingway: Selected Letters, 1917–1961*. New York: Scribners, 1981.

Barker, Thomas. *Barker's Delight: or, The Art of Angling*. London: Humphrey Moselye, 1659. Reprinted in *Three Books on Fishing (1599–1659) Associated with* The Compleat Angler (1653) by Izaak Walton. Gainesville, Fla.: Scholars' Facsimiles and Reprints, 1962.

Barrett, Richmond. "Babes in the Bois." *Harper's Magazine*, May 1928, 724–36.

Barton, William E. *The Autobiography of William E. Barton*. Indianapolis: Bobbs-Merrill, 1932.

————. *The Gospel of the Average Man*. Oak Park: Puritan Press, 1911.

Beegel, Susan, ed. *Hemingway's Neglected Short Fiction: New Perspectives*. Ann Arbor, Mich.: UMI Research Press, 1989.

Bell, Millicent. "*A Farewell to Arms:* Pseudoautobiography and Personal Metaphor." In *Ernest Hemingway: The Writer in Context*, ed. James Nagel, 107–28. Madison: University of Wisconsin Press, 1984.

Blair, Walter. "Huck and Tom among the Indians." *Life*, December 20, 1968, 32–50.

Bovie, Smith Palmer. *Virgil's Georgics: A Modern English Verse Translation*. Chicago: University of Chicago Press, 1956.

Brasch, James D., and Joseph Sigman. *Hemingway's Library: A Composite Record*. New York: Garland, 1981.

Brenner, Gerry. *Concealments in Hemingway's Works*. Columbus: Ohio State University Press, 1983.

————. "From 'Sepi Jingan' to 'The Mother of a Queen': Hemingway's Three Epistemologic Formulas for Short Fiction." In *New Critical Ap-*

Bibliography

proaches to the Short Stories of Ernest Hemingway, ed. Jackson J. Benson, 156–71. Durham: Duke University Press, 1990.

Bruccoli, Matthew J., ed. *Ernest Hemingway's Apprenticeship: Oak Park, 1916–1917*. New York: Microcard Editions, 1971.

————. *Scott and Ernest: The Authority of Failure and the Authority of Success*. New York: Random House, 1978.

Bundy, James F. *Fall from Grace: Religion and the Communal Ideal in Two Suburban Villages, 1870–1917*. Brooklyn, N.Y.: Carlson Publishing, 1991.

Burnham, James. "Incompleat Angler." *New International*, March 1938, 92–93.

Cole, Arthur Charles. *The Era of the Civil War, 1848–1870*. Springfield: Illinois Centennial Commission, 1919.

Cooper, John R. *The Art of the Compleat Angler*. Durham: Duke University Press, 1968.

Cowley, Malcolm. "Hemingway's Wound—And Its Consequences for American Literature." *Georgia Review* 38 (Summer 1984): 223–39.

————. Introduction to the Viking Portable Library *Hemingway*, vii–xxiv. New York: Viking, 1944.

Donaldson, Scott. "Censorship and *A Farewell to Arms*." *Studies in American Fiction* 19 (1991): 85–93.

————. "The Wooing of Ernest Hemingway." *American Literature* 53 (1982): 691–710.

Fenton, Charles. "No Money for the Kingbird: Hemingway's Prizefighter Stories." *American Quarterly* 4 (Winter 1952): 339–50.

Fiedler, Leslie. *Love and Death in the American Novel*. New York: Criterion Books, 1960.

Fitzgerald, F. Scott. "How to Waste Material, A Note on My Generation." *Bookman* 63 (May 1926): 262–65. Reprinted in *Ernest Hemingway: The Critical Reception*, ed. Robert O. Stephens, 17–19. New York: Burt Franklin, 1977.

Fleming, Robert E. "Hemingway's Dr. Adams—Saint or Sinner?" *Arizona Quarterly* 39 (Summer 1983): 101–10.

Flora, Joseph M. *Hemingway's Nick Adams*. Baton Rouge: Louisiana State University Press, 1982.

Foster, David. *The Scientific Angler: Being a General and Instructive Work on Artistic Angling*. Comp. his sons and ed. William C. Harris. New York: Orange Judd, 1883.

Geismar, Maxwell, ed. *The Ring Lardner Reader*. New York: Charles Scribners Sons, 1963.

Grebstein, Sheldon N. *Hemingway's Craft*. Carbondale: Southern Illinois University Press, 1973.

Green, Gregory. " 'A Matter of Color': Hemingway's Criticism of Race Prejudice." *Hemingway Review* 1 (Fall 1981): 27–32.

Grey, Zane. "A Trout Fisherman's Inferno." In *Zane Grey: Outdoorsman*, ed. George Reiger, 282–91. Englewood Cliffs, N.J.: Prentice-Hall, 1972.

Griffin, Peter. *Along with Youth: Hemingway, the Early Years*. Oxford and New York: Oxford University Press, 1985.

Grimes, Larry E. *The Religious Design of Hemingway's Early Fiction*. Ann Arbor, Mich.: UMI Research Press, 1985.

Hanneman, Audre. *Ernest Hemingway: A Comprehensive Bibliography*. Princeton: Princeton University Press, 1987.

Hart, Irving Harlow. "The Most Popular Authors of Fiction in the Post-War Period, 1919–1926." *Publisher's Weekly*, March 12, 1927, 1045–52.

Helmle, Robert K. "Boyhood Recollections of Ernest Hemingway and His Father." In *The Toe River Anthology*, ed. Francis Hulme, 83–94. Burnsville, N.C.: Toe River Arts Council, 1979.

Hemingway, Ernest. *Across the River and Into the Trees*. New York: Scribners, 1970.

———. "American Bohemians in Paris." *Toronto Star Weekly*, March 25, 1922. In *By-Line: Ernest Hemingway*, ed. William White, 23–25. New York: Scribners, 1967.

———. "The Art of the Short Story." *Paris Review*, Spring 1981, 85–102.

———. "The Best Rainbow Trout Fishing." *Toronto Star Weekly*, August 28, 1920. Reprinted in *Dateline Toronto: The Complete Toronto Star Dispatches, 1920–1924*, ed. William White, 50–52. New York: Scribners, 1985.

———. "Big Two-Hearted River." *Field and Stream*, May 1954, 45–48, 96–105.

———. *The Complete Short Stories of Ernest Hemingway: The Finca Vigia Edition*. New York: Scribners, 1987.

———. *Death in the Afternoon*. New York: Scribners, 1932.

———. *A Farewell to Arms*. New York: Scribners, 1929.

———. *The Fifth Column and the First Forty-Nine Stories*. New York: Scribners, 1930.

———. *For Whom the Bell Tolls*. New York: Scribners, 1940.

———. *in our time*. Paris: Three Mountains Press, 1924; Bloomfield Hills, Mich.: Broccoli Clark, 1977.

———. *Islands in the Stream*. New York: Scribners, 1970.

———. *A Moveable Feast*. New York: Scribners, 1964.

———. *The Nick Adams Stories*, ed. Philip Young. New York: Scribners, 1972.

———. "Out in the Stream: A Cuban Letter." *Esquire*, August 1934, 19, 156, 168. Reprinted in *By-Line: Ernest Hemingway*, ed. William White, 172–78. New York: Scribners, 1967.

———. *The Short Stories of Ernest Hemingway*. New York: Collier Books, 1986.

———. *The Short Stories of Ernest Hemingway: The First Forty-Nine Stories and the Play "The Fifth Column."* New York: Modern Library, 1938.

———. *The Sun Also Rises*. New York: Scribners, 1926.

———. *Three Stories and Ten Poems*. Paris: Contact Publishing Company, 1923.

———. *Winner Take Nothing*. New York: Scribners, 1933.

Hemingway, Leicester. *My Brother, Ernest Hemingway*. 2d ed. Miami Beach, Fla.: Winchester House, 1980.

Bibliography

Hemingway, Mary Welsh. *How It Was*. New York: Alfred Knopf, 1976.

Hemingway, Patricia S. *The Hemingways: Past and Present and Allied Families*. Baltimore: Gateway Press, 1988.

Hovey, Richard B. *Hemingway: The Inward Terrain*. Seattle: University of Washington Press, 1968.

Howells, William Dean. *Selected Letters of W. D. Howells*, ed. George Arms and Christoph K. Lohmann. Boston: Twayne, 1979.

Hutchison, William R. *The Modernist Impulse in American Protestantism*. Cambridge: Harvard University Press, 1976.

Isabelle, Julanne. *Hemingway's Religious Experience*. New York: Vantage Press, 1964.

Jameson, Fredric. *Marxism and Form: Twentieth-Century Dialectical Theories of Literature*. Princeton: Princeton University Press, 1974.

Johns-Heine, Patricke, and Hans H. Gerth. "Values in Mass Periodical Fiction, 1921–1940." In *Mass Culture: The Popular Arts in America*, ed. Bernard Rosenberg and David Manning White, 226–34. London: Collier-Macmillan, 1957.

Johnson, David R. " 'The Last Good Country': Again the End of Something." In *New Critical Approaches to the Short Stories of Ernest Hemingway*, ed. Jackson J. Benson, 314–20. Durham: Duke University Press, 1990.

Kert, Bernice. *The Hemingway Women*. New York and London: Norton, 1983.

Kuklick, Bruce, ed. *William James, Writings 1902–1910*. New York: Library of America, 1987.

Lamb, Robert Paul. "Fishing for Stories: What 'Big Two-Hearted River' Is Really About." *Modern Fiction Studies* 37 (Summer 1991): 161–81.

Lang, Andrew. Introduction to *The Compleat Angler*. London and New York: J. M. Dent and E. P. Dutton, 1906.

Lewis, R. W. B. "Who's Papa?" *New Republic*, December 2, 1985, 33–34.

Lewis, Robert W. " 'Long Time Ago Good, Now No Good': Hemingway's Indian Stories." In *New Critical Approaches to the Short Stories of Ernest Hemingway*, ed. Jackson Benson, 200–212. Durham: Duke University Press, 1990.

Lynn, Kenneth. *Hemingway*. New York: Simon and Schuster, 1987.

———. "Hemingway's Private War." *Commentary*, July 1981, 24–33. Reprinted in *The Air-Line to Seattle: Studies in Literary and Historical Writing about America*, 108–31. Chicago: University of Chicago Press, 1983.

———. "Hemingway's Wars." *New Republic*, January 20, 1986, 6, 40.

Maziarka, Cynthia, and Donald Vogel, Jr., eds. *Hemingway at Oak Park High School: The High School Writings of Ernest Hemingway, 1916–1917*. Oak Park, Ill.: Oak Park and River Forest High School, 1993.

Mellow, James. *Hemingway: A Life without Consequences*. New York: Houghton Mifflin, 1992.

Meyers, Jeffrey. *Hemingway: A Biography*. New York: Harper and Row, 1985.

———, ed. *Hemingway: The Critical Heritage*. Boston: Routledge and Kegan Paul, 1983.

Miko, Stephen. "The River, the Iceberg, and the Shit-Detector." *Criticism* 33 (Fall 1991): 503–25.

Miller, Madelaine Hemingway. *Ernie*. New York: Crown, 1975.

Mitchell, Sally. *Dinah Mulock Craik*. Boston: Twayne, 1983.

Montgomery, Constance Cappel. *Hemingway in Michigan*. New York: Fleet Publishing, 1966.

Mulock, Miss [Dinah Maria Craik]. *John Halifax, Gentleman*. New York: Thomas Y. Crowell, 1897.

Nagel, James, ed. *Ernest Hemingway: The Writer in Context*. Madison: University of Wisconsin Press, 1984.

———. "Hemingway and the Italian Legacy." In *Hemingway in Love and War*, ed. Henry S. Villard and James Nagel, 197–269. Boston: Northeastern University Press, 1989.

Notpoh, Nagrom. "In Praise of M. Barkers Excellent Book of Angling." In Thomas Barker, *Barker's Delight: or, The Art of Angling*. London: Humphrey Moselye, 1659. Reprinted in *Three Books on Fishing (1599–1659) Associated with* The Complete Angler *(1653) by Izaak Walton*. Gainesville, Fla.: Scholars' Facsimiles and Reprints, 1962.

Oak Park and River Forest High School: 1873–1976. Oak Park, Ill.: Osla Graphics, n.d.

Oldsey, Bernard. "Hemingway's Beginnings and Endings." *College Literature* 7 (Fall 1980): 213–38.

Orton, Vrest. "Some Notes Bibliographical and Otherwise on the Books on Ernest Hemingway." *Publisher's Weekly*, February 15, 1930, 884–86.

Pinsker, Sanford. "Revisionism with Rancor: The Threat of the Neoconservative Critics." *Georgia Review* 38 (Summer 1984): 255–56.

Plimpton, George, ed. *Writers at Work: The Paris Review Interviews*. 2d ser. New York: Penguin, 1977.

Preminger, Alex, Frank J. Warnke, and O. B. Hardison, Jr., eds. *Princeton Encyclopedia of Poetry and Poetics*. Enlarged ed. Princeton: Princeton University Press, 1974.

Reynolds, Michael S. *Critical Essays on Ernest Hemingway's* In Our Time. Boston: G. K. Hall, 1983.

———. *Hemingway: The American Homecoming*. Cambridge, Mass.: Blackwell, 1992.

———. *Hemingway: The Paris Years*. Oxford and New York: Blackwell, 1989.

———. *Hemingway's First War: The Making of* A Farewell to Arms. Princeton: Princeton University Press, 1976.

———. *Hemingway's Reading 1910–1940: An Inventory*. Princeton: Princeton University Press, 1981.

———. "Macomber: An Old Oak Park Name." *Hemingway Review* 3 (Fall 1983): 28–29.

———. *The Young Hemingway*. New York: Blackwell, 1986.

Ross, Lillian. *Portrait of Hemingway*. New York: Simon and Schuster, 1961.

Sanford, Marcelline Hemingway. *At the Hemingways: A Family Portrait*. Boston: Little, Brown, 1961.

Schleden, Ina Mae, and Marion Rawls Herzog, eds. *Ernest Hemingway as*

Bibliography

Recalled by His High School Contemporaries. Oak Park, Ill.: Historical Society of Oak Park and River Forest, 1973.

Smith, B. J. " 'Big Two-Hearted River': The Artist and the Art." *Studies in Short Fiction* 20 (Spring–Summer 1983): 129–32.

Smith, Paul. "Hemingway's Apprentice Fiction: 1919–1921." *American Literature* 58 (December 1986): 574–88.

———, ed. *A Reader's Guide to the Short Stories of Ernest Hemingway*. Boston: G. K. Hall, 1989.

———. "The Tenth Indian and the Thing Left Out." In *Ernest Hemingway: The Writer in Context*, ed. James Nagel, 53–74. Madison: University of Wisconsin Press, 1984.

Sojka, Gregory S. *Ernest Hemingway: The Angler as Artist*. New York: Peter Lang, 1985.

Spanier, Sandra Whipple. "Hemingway's 'The Last Good Country' and *The Catcher in the Rye:* More Than a Family Resemblance." *Studies in Short Fiction* 19 (1982): 35–43.

Spilka, Mark. *Hemingway's Quarrel with Androgyny*. Lincoln: University of Nebraska Press, 1990.

St. John, Donald. "Hemingway and Prudence." *Connecticut Review* 5 (April 1972): 78–84.

Stephens, Robert O., ed. *Ernest Hemingway: The Critical Reception*. New York: Burt Franklin, 1977.

Svoboda, Frederic Joseph. *Hemingway and* The Sun Also Rises: *The Crafting of a Style*. Lawrence: University Press of Kansas, 1983.

Swartzlander, Susan. "Uncle Charles in Michigan." In *Hemingway's Neglected Short Fiction: New Perspectives*, ed. Susan Beegel, 31–42. Ann Arbor, Mich.: UMI Research Press, 1989.

Tate, Allen. "Good Prose." *The Nation*, February 10, 1926, 160–62.

Villard, Henry S., and James Nagel. *Hemingway in Love and War: The Lost Diary of Agnes von Kurowsky*. Boston: Northeastern University Press, 1989.

Wagner, Linda W. [Wagner-Martin, Linda]. " 'Proud and Friendly and Gently: Women in Hemingway's Early Fiction." In *Ernest Hemingway: The Papers of a Writer*, ed. Bernard Oldsey, 63–71. New York: Garland, 1981.

Walton, Izaak. *The Compleat Angler 1653–1676*. Ed. Jonquil Bevan. Oxford: Clarendon Press, 1983.

Ward, William S. *A Literary History of Kentucky*. Knoxville: University of Tennessee Press, 1988.

Westbrook, Max. "Grace under Pressure: Hemingway and the Summer of 1920." In *Ernest Hemingway: The Writer in Context*, ed. James Nagel, 77–106. Madison: University of Wisconsin Press, 1984.

———. "Text, Ritual, and Memory: Hemingway's 'Big Two-Hearted River.' " *North Dakota Quarterly* 60 (Summer 1992): 14–25.

White, William, ed. *By-Line: Ernest Hemingway*. New York: Scribners, 1967.

Wilson, Edmund. "Ernest Hemingway: Bourdon Gauge of Morale." *Atlantic Monthly*, July 1939, 36–46.

Wylie, Elinor. "The Two Glass Doors: Wherein the Past and Future become Transparent to a Perplexed Young Lady." *Vanity Fair,* May 1923, 67, 102.

Young, Philip. "Big World Out There." In *The Short Stories of Ernest Hemingway: Critical Essays,* ed. Jackson J. Benson, 29–44. Durham: Duke University Press, 1975.

———. *Ernest Hemingway.* New York: Rinehart, 1952.

———. "Posthumous Hemingway and Nicholas Adams." In *Hemingway in Our Time,* ed. Richard Astro and Jackson J. Benson, 13–23. Corvallis: Oregon State University Press, 1974.

CONTRIBUTORS

CARLOS AZEVEDO is an Associate Professor in the Department of Anglo-American Studies at the University of Oporto, Portugal, where he founded the American Studies program. He has lectured on American literature and culture since 1974. Among his publications are *Between the Real and Abstraction: The Narrative Fiction of Ernest Hemingway, F. Scott Fitzgerald and* The Great Gatsby: *An Encounter with The Modern Temper,* and *Hemingway in Portugal.* He is a member of the Hemingway Society and the Portuguese Association for Anglo-American Studies.

MORRIS BUSKE was born in Wisconsin, pursued undergraduate work at the River Falls State Teachers College, and completed course work for a Ph.D. in History at the University of Wisconsin. In 1940, he joined the faculty of the Oak Park and River Forest High School, where some of his colleagues were teachers and friends of Ernest Hemingway. In 1984, after his retirement, he and his late wife, Dorothy, founded The Ernest Hemingway Foundation of Oak Park, which he has served as chairman and then as historian. His publications include reviews, articles, learning guides, a world history textbook, and *Lovely Walloona,* a play about the relationship between Ernest Hemingway and his parents.

JOHN J. FENSTERMAKER is a Professor of English at Florida State University. He is a past president of the South Atlantic Association of Departments of English and the Florida College English Association and has served on the MLA Delegate Assembly. A Victorian scholar by training, he has written books on Charles Dickens and John Forster, and he collaborated with Richard D. Altick on *The Art of Literary Research* (1993). Adding to his earlier work on American writers, focusing on Ralph Waldo Emerson and F. Scott Fitzgerald, he is at work on a comprehensive Hemingway chronology.

LARRY E. GRIMES holds the Gresham chair in humanities at Bethany College in West Virginia. He received a Master's of Divinity from Yale Divinity School and a Ph.D. in theology and literature from Emory University. Among his publications is *The Religious Design of Hemingway's Early Fiction.*

JUDY HEN is a doctoral candidate in the Department of English and American Literature at Tel Aviv University, where she is completing a dissertation on the cultural influences behind Hemingway's early fiction.

Contributors

DAVID MARUT holds a master's degree in English from Northern Illinois University and pursued doctoral work at the University of Georgia. He won the Arnold B. Fox Critical Studies Award from Northern Illinois University for his work on Ralph Ellison's *Invisible Man*. In 1994 he presented a paper on Frank Norris at the American Literature Association conference in San Diego.

GEORGE MONTEIRO is a Professor of English and of Portuguese and Brazilian studies at Brown University. His works include editions of the letters of Henry James, Henry Adams, William Dean Howells, and John Hay; a critical study of the poetry of Robert Frost; and *Critical Essays on Ernest Hemingway's* A Farewell to Arms.

JAMES NAGEL, J. O. Eidson Distinguished Professor of American Literature at the University of Georgia, founded the scholarly journal *Studies in American Fiction* and edited it for twenty years. He is the general editor of the *Critical Essays on American Literature* series, published by Macmillan in New York, a program that now contains over 130 volumes. He is also a past president of the Hemingway Society. Among his fifteen books are *Stephen Crane and Literary Impressionism, Hemingway: The Writer in Context, Critical Essays on* The Sun Also Rises, and *Hemingway in Love and War,* which was selected by the *New York Times* as one of the outstanding books of 1989.

MARY ANNE O'NEAL is a doctoral candidate in American literature and women's studies at the University of Georgia. She has been a lecturer at Western Carolina University. Her dissertation focuses on three women writers from New Orleans: Kate Chopin, Alice Dunbar Nelson, and Grace King.

MICHAEL REYNOLDS, Professor of English and Associate Dean for Research at North Carolina State University, is a founding member of the Hemingway Society and a Hemingway biographer. He is currently finishing *Hemingway: The 1930s*, the fourth volume in his projected five-volume biography. The first three volumes were *The Young Hemingway; Hemingway: The Paris Years;* and *Hemingway: The American Homecoming.*

ABBY H. P. WERLOCK, Associate Professor of English at St. Olaf College, received her doctorate in American Studies at the University of Sussex, England. She has received fellowships from the National Endowment for the Humanities and the Joyce Foundation of Chicago as well as the 1992 Bob Casey award for her article on Steinbeck and Faulkner in *San Jose Studies*. She is coauthor of *Tillie Olsen* and editor of *British Women Writing Fiction*. Her current projects involve a book on the composition of Hemingway's *To Have and Have Not* and a collection of essays, *Hemingway's Fictional Women.*

226

INDEX

Index

Index

Index

Index